BURN THE WHITE FLAG

CHARLES NIEMAN

BURN THE WHITE FLAG

HOW TO FIGHT FOR AN ABUNDANT LIFE

Fedd Books
P.O. Box 341973
Austin, TX 78734

www.thefeddagency.com

Published in association with The Fedd Agency, Inc., a literary agency.

ISBN: 978-1-949784-18-3
eISBN: 978-1-949784-19-0

Printed in the United States of America

First Edition 15 14 13 12 11 / 10 9 8 7 6 5 4 3 2

CONTENTS

INTRODUCTION

Dr. Whitney Smith (1940-2016) has been widely recognized as the world's foremost vexillologist, which simply means he was a scholar of flags. His passion for flags and what they represent was truly inspiring; he dedicated his life to the study of flags throughout history and around the world, collecting over a quarter of a million documents and flag-related artifacts in his lifetime, which are now housed at the University of Texas at Austin. Whenever Dr. Smith was asked why he took flags so seriously, his standard reply was: "People kill for flags. People die for flags. It is incumbent on us to try to understand how a piece of cloth can incarnate that power."[1]

He's right. Flags have power. Throughout history, countless armies have marched, sailed, and flown into war while proudly bearing the flag of their respective nations. In life and in death, the flag represents a soldier's loyalty, sacrifice, and allegiance. Soldiers and citizens alike are inspired by the sight of the flag. Francis Scott Key famously wrote the national anthem of the United States of America, "The Star-Spangled Banner," after seeing the American flag flying over Fort McHenry during a battle with the British in 1814.

But there is a flag no one writes songs or poems about. No one follows it into battle or gives their life to protect it. It doesn't inspire feelings of pride, but rather of shame. This flag isn't carefully folded or proudly unfurled. As a matter of fact, I've been told no army even carries it into battle. It's the white flag of surrender.

For thousands of years, the white flag has been a symbol of defeat. It is a call for truce and ceasefire. When an army waves the white flag, they are giving up. They are exchanging their freedom for survival; they are exchanging their national pride for subjection to a foreign power. That's why armies don't carry white flags. There's not a white flag anywhere in the division, in the regiment, in the company, in the platoon, or on the ship. When they go to war, there is no plan to surrender. There is no plan to give up, so they don't take a white flag. In the Persian Gulf War, many Iraqi army officers made their soldiers hand over any white article of clothing, including undershirts and socks, to avoid the temptation of surrendering to American forces.[2]

I believe there is a time for truce in some wars. Surrender can save lives and restore peace. But in the *Christian walk*, in the spiritual war going on around us, surrender cannot be an option. Surrendering in the Christian walk means *to not fully live out the purpose and calling that God has for you.* God has given you everything you need to live life to the fullest and anything short of that is surrender. We are in a fight to the finish, a battle for our lives, and we cannot resort to waving a white flag. Why? First, because we only have one life. And second, because we are following Jesus, and we cannot be defeated. In Him we are more than conquerors, the Bible says (Romans 8:37). Defeat is not in our future, so the white flag should not be in our bags. It should not be packed in our thinking, in our hearts, in our souls, in our families.

If there is a white flag somewhere in your life, I want to encourage you to burn that flag. Through this book, I am going to walk with you through what you will be fighting against as you remove the thoughts of giving in. We are going to challenge and change the urges of giving up and surrendering, of losing our hearts and our souls. Through the story of the Israelites entering the Promised Land, as well as other biblical stories, we will look at what it takes in order to fully realize what God has in store for us.

Let me say from the outset that I have struggled with thoughts of giving up as much as anyone—and maybe more than many. I know what it is like to want to wave the white flag. I have faced the loss of a loved one and close friends. I've fought through four back surgeries and the pain and risk that go along with them. As a pastor, I've endured lies about myself and our church. I've been betrayed by people I thought were my friends. I've watched things I fought for be lost overnight. I've labored year in and year out over four decades to serve people and serve God, and there have been many times when it seemed my labor was not bearing fruit. I can't count how many times I have thought about quitting on life, on my dreams, on my hopes, and on my purpose.

Yet, here I am! I'm not perfect, but I'm still here. I've made mistakes, but I'm still here. I haven't waved the white flag, and I don't intend to now. I'd like to help inspire you in your own fight. I don't pretend to have all the answers, but, over the years, I have learned quite a few things about life with Jesus. I've seen the rewards of endurance and faith, of fighting for my purpose. I've seen God's promise of restoration in my life fulfilled.

This concept of not surrendering, of persevering to the end, has become a deeply held value in my life simply because I have thought about quitting so many times. But I haven't quit. That's what matters. God wants to help you win your fight. Even if life has knocked you down, even if you've made some poor choices (because we all have), even if others have told you that you'll never succeed, there is a future for you! God wants to give you a life better than you could imagine. As the war is raging around you, take courage and burn the white flag.

ONE

RUNNING TO WIN

FAITH AND ENDURANCE

Hebrews 11 is one of the most famous chapters in the Bible, and with good reason: it lists heroes and heroines of faith whose lives inspire us to persevere. People like Noah, Abraham, Sarah, Isaac, Jacob, Moses, Rahab, Gideon, Samson, David, and Samuel. People "who through faith conquered kingdoms, enforced justice, obtained promises, stopped the mouths of lions, quenched the power of fire, escaped the edge of the sword, were made strong out of weakness, became mighty in war, and put foreign armies to flight" (Hebrews 11:33-34). People who were willing to be "tortured, refusing to accept release, so that they might rise again to a better life" (verse 35). People who fought, people who didn't lose faith, people who never waved the white flag.

The writer of Hebrews begins chapter 12 by saying, "Therefore, since we are surrounded by so great a cloud of witnesses . . ." (Hebrews 12:1). In other words, those people are our role models; their lives serve as examples for how to walk out our faith. Their lives bore witness to the power of the Word, the power of faith, the power of guts and grit, the power of determination and passion, the power of perseverance. They aren't just legendary heroes of the Bible; they are our spiritual ancestors. We come from a long line of winners. We are not going to cave in or become cowards, because just like our forefathers, we can find strength in our faith in God and stay firm to the end.

The author of Hebrews continues, ". . . let us also lay aside every weight, and sin which clings so closely, and let us run with endurance the race that is set before us" (Hebrews 12:1). All of us are running in this race called life. The apostle Paul used the same racing metaphor to talk about the Christian walk, "Do you not know that in a race all the runners run, but only one receives the prize? So run that you may obtain it" (1 Corinthians 9:24). We are told to run the race *with endurance*, and we are told to run *to obtain the prize*. This is not an easy race to win though. We face constant pressure from the devil and from the world around us; we face two recurring pressures: one is to quit the race and the other is to settle for losing. To quit the race means to give up on life. It means to just sit back and let life dominate us instead of going out and fighting to obtain the life God wants us to have. And to lose the race means to accept just finishing, rather than attaining the abundant life God offers us. The temptation to surrender is sometimes disguised as the temptation to settle, to make do with less than what God has put in your heart and in His Word for you to enjoy. There is recurring pressure to live with mediocrity. That is a form of waving the white flag, and we need to root that mentality out of our lives.

REJECTING MEDIOCRITY

Mediocrity means *average or commonplace*. To be average is to be right in the middle of the pack: not too high, not too low. It means you don't stand out for the wrong reasons, but you don't stand out for the right reasons, either. We are not called to be *ordinary*. Ordinary doesn't sound so bad at first—except God didn't call us to that. He called us to live abundant lives and significant lives. Jesus said in John 10:10, "I came that they may have life and have it abundantly." Notice He didn't say, "I came that they may have life more ordinary." And yet, there is pressure on our lives to do exactly that. Jesus did not come to give us a barely adequate life, a life of just barely making it. That's not what He intends for you or for me, and I don't believe we should accept it.

There's so much pressure placed upon us to accept a commonplace life. Have you ever had a conversation like this?

"How is your marriage doing?"

"Well, I guess it's as good as anybody else's."

Really? That's good enough for you? Or how about this one:

"How is your relationship with your kids?"

"I don't know. It's okay, I guess. Pretty normal."

Normal is not setting the bar very high, my friend! Why are we willing to accept ordinary? We need to get John 10:10 into our hearts, minds, and wills. We need to make it personal. Jesus did not come to give you or me life that is normal, average, or mediocre. That's not what He has for you or your family. You need to believe that Jesus came to give you abundant life, a better life than you ever dreamed of, a life that is anything but commonplace or barely adequate.

It might be hard to do that if you come from a background of ordinariness. I'm not referring to your financial situation growing up, the home you lived in, or the school you went to. You can be well-off and still be ordinary. And you can struggle financially and yet be extraordinary and full of life. Extraordinary is found in the heart, not in the bank account. I'm talking about a mentality of mediocrity that might have been instilled in you by family members, friends, mentors, and bosses. I'm talking about the experiences that formed your philosophy of life. Maybe in your childhood and in your family background you were taught not to make waves—to be content with the status quo, to be satisfied with barely adequate. You were told, "This is who we are. This is how we live. Don't try to change it. Accept it." You were taught to know your place, and, decades later, you're still in that place. God is calling you to an abundant life; He has so much planned for your life.

That's why God tells us not just to finish, but to win. He tells us to run for the prize. We need to toughen up, stay the course, and finish well. We can all win, but it requires effort, passion, perseverance, and discipline. It requires making the decision to give it your all and to never give up, to never settle for second best. It's going to get hard at times, but that's okay. You need to know that. Hard is not bad—it's just hard. We were made for this. God is with us, and His strength is perfected in our weakness. The only way we lose is if we quit or if we settle.

I'm glad the verse doesn't say, "run the race with intelligence," because I'm not that smart. I'm glad it doesn't say, "run the race with luck," because luck isn't a very reliable strategy. I'm glad it doesn't say, "run the race better than everyone else," because I'm not better than everyone else. And I'm glad He didn't say, "run the race without ever messing up," because I have a track record of mistakes. God didn't say any of those things. He said to run the race with endurance. That's not only the key to finishing, it's the key to finishing well—to winning. And the good news is this: endurance is available to us all. No one is naturally gifted with endurance. No one is born with endurance. We choose it. We grow in it. We develop it.

THE FAITH OF HEROES

If you take a look at the backstories of the heroes in Hebrews 11, you'll notice a common denominator. They were all completely human. They made mistakes—big mistakes. They had weak moments. They doubted God and themselves. Many of them came from very difficult or dysfunctional backgrounds. Clearly, being a hero of faith is not about having a perfect resumé.

But they had one other commonality: they finished well. When they fell, they got back up. When they made mistakes, they owned their errors and got back in the race. And now they are immortalized in a chapter dedicated to illustrating faith. That should tell us something about faith. Faith is less about perfection and more about patience. It's less about not having weakness and more about persevering in spite of weakness. If faith is an inner conviction, endurance is an external action. True faith will always produce endurance, and endurance is the proof of faith.

Many years ago, I found myself in a very difficult spot. It was a real pressure cooker. Our church was fourteen years old. We had experienced steady growth for a solid decade. We had always been in the black in our finances, we had purchased land and built new church facilities, and the future was exciting. Then almost overnight, due to circumstances beyond our control, we began to experience a very difficult season as a church. Attendance dropped, giving dropped—and it stayed that way for three years. Our church finances were in the red every month, and, no matter what we did, we couldn't seem to right the ship.

My wife and I had two small kids at the time, and we went months without receiving a salary. The stress and pressure were unlike anything I had ever experienced. I started having chest pains; my hair was falling out. Honestly, I don't know how we survived. At one point, without telling anyone, I even had an appraiser come in and give us a fire-sale appraisal of the church land and building, because I was almost sure we were going to have to declare bankruptcy. I had personally signed to guarantee the church note, so the situation was looking very bad for the church and for my family. I remember thinking time after time that I wanted to escape, I wanted to quit, I wanted to run. I didn't know how to continue, and quitting seemed like the only option.

Then one day, out of the blue, something happened that changed everything. I was driving down the freeway. I still remember the exact spot where I was when I felt like God spoke to my heart. It had been months, maybe years, since I had heard His voice like that. He simply said, "You know what to do. Do it."

And I did know. I can't explain how, but I knew.

I drove to the church and went to my office. In my desk I had a box of cards with Scripture verses on them, and I took them out. I began to read them out loud and declare them in faith. That might sound odd, but the Bible says in 1 John 5:4, "this is the victory that has overcome the world—our faith." I knew what God was saying to me. It wasn't the fact we were a great church that was going to pull us through. It wasn't our innocence or our goodness. It wasn't because I was a nice guy who had done nothing wrong. It wasn't my preaching or our ministries. It wasn't business savvy. Those are all good, necessary things, but they weren't enough to see us to the end. *It was faith in God.*

And let's be honest: that simply means it was *God.* My faith wasn't so strong at the time, but God was and is and always will be enough. I just had to remember that. I started reading those verses out loud three times a day. It was like a prescription for the health of my spirit. Something changed in me, and something changed in the atmosphere.

That was in January. That month, for the first time since the crisis started three years earlier, we broke even. In February, we went back in the red, but barely. That month I also met a pastor named Tommy Barnett, who to this day is my pastor and my friend. He became a strength and source of wisdom, and I owe him so much. In March, we were back in the black, and we haven't been in the red since. That was nearly thirty years ago.

I still remember the feelings of doubt, fear, and inadequacy. The desperation. The hopelessness. I remember wanting to quit. But during those times, before things started to turn for the better, I came to a realization. It didn't feel like a very positive thought at the time, but as I looked back, I realized it saved me from making dumb decisions and waving the white flag in tough times. The realization was this: quitting wouldn't help. I remember asking myself, *Will my life get better if I quit? Will everything improve if I surrender to the circumstances? If I throw up my hands in disgust and just give up, are things suddenly going to get better?*

I realized the answer was no. If I were to give up, if I were to surrender to Satan, if I were to surrender to the circumstances, if I were to surrender to the world, if I were to give in to the world's philosophy about life instead of living according to God's Word, if I were to decide it was too hard and that I was going to go live like the world lives—nothing would improve. My family wouldn't get better. My future wouldn't get better. My relationship with God wouldn't get better. I remember thinking, *So why would I give up?* The only logical reason to surrender would be if my life would genuinely get better as a result of surrendering. But if not, why surrender? Why become a prisoner?

I know it feels like the pressure is too much at times. But take an honest look at your situation. What will you give up by giving up? Is it worth it? Will you really be happier or more at ease? Most likely, the answer is no. If the answer is yes, then maybe you were doing the wrong thing in the first place. That's a valid conclusion, by the way. Sometimes we can get overcommitted or distracted from what we are supposed to be doing, and we feel overwhelmed because we are doing things we don't need to do. Maybe you need to dial back your activity in certain areas so you can focus on what really matters.

In my experience, however, most of our goals are good goals, and most of our activities are good activities. They're just not always easy. We feel like quitting on a regular basis. That's normal, but don't make a decision based on fatigue or frustration. It's just a season. Stay firm, and you'll make it to the end.

I've also noticed that the temptation to give up is often greatest right before the biggest breakthrough. We don't realize how close we are to the end, and we get discouraged. It's like the guy who swam three-quarters of the way across a lake, decided he couldn't make it, and turned around and swam back. In the long run, quitting is usually harder than finishing well.

As we continue to talk about the tools and traits needed to run the race and fight the battle of faith to win, we will look at the Israelites and their journey to the Promised Land. In the book of Exodus, we read that God promised His people, the Israelites, that He would take them out of bondage and into a prosperous land. God wanted to give His children an abundant life, just as He does for us today. From the Israelites, we can learn the dos and don'ts of running this race and standing firm in the spiritual war going on around us. The foundation is to keep faith and to always turn to Jesus.

This race matters, and it's the race Jesus is helping you win. Don't let any voice drown out Jesus' voice. Don't look to them more than you look to Jesus. They don't know what's in your future, and honestly, neither do you. But Jesus does, and as long as you look to Him, you'll find the strength you need to endure and win.

TWO

ARMOR UP

FIGHT APATHY WITH GRIT

The spiritual war going on around us is constant and taxing. In order to fight well, we need the armor and tools that will ensure our victory. In Ephesians 6:10-18, Paul talks about walking through life with the whole armor of God. It's a wonderful description of the different strategies and tools we have at our disposal in our resistance against the devil. Paul talks about the belt of truth, the breastplate of righteousness, the footwear of the gospel of peace, the shield of faith, the helmet of salvation, and the sword of the Spirit. Verse 18 concludes the section with this: "praying at all times in the Spirit, with all prayer and supplication. To that end, keep alert with all perseverance, making supplication for all the saints." In other words, while these elements of armor are essential, there are two overarching qualities that make them work: prayer and perseverance.

The Christian life isn't about having faith once in a while, but about persevering in faith. It's not about having the truth once in a while, but about persevering in the truth. You are protected by God, but you must work with Him and not against Him. Your daily battles must be surrounded by prayer and dependence on God.

The word *perseverance* in this passage has a variety of meanings, including *endurance, patience, long-suffering, persistence in a course of action, purpose, and doggedness.* I like that word *doggedness.* It literally means *having characteristics of a dog,*[3] which brings up images of a bulldog who won't let go, or a bloodhound resolutely following a scent, or a dog whose loyalty to his master is never-ending. Perseverance also means to be resolute and unyielding in holding on in following a course of action. It refers to activity maintained in spite of difficulty; steadfast and long-continued application. That's the long definition of perseverance. The short definition, the Texas definition, is *grit.*

Grit can be defined as *firmness of character; indomitable spirit; a spirit that will not be conquered; resolution; fortitude, strength of will.* It has the idea of toughness, tenacity, determination, and endurance. Grit means you have guts. You have strength of character. There is a toughness to your life. Grit says, "I've started this, and I'm going to finish it. I'm going to be firm. I'm going to stay committed. I'm going to stay strong in my relationship with God and others. I'm going to stay faithful to my marriage and my family. I'm going to live by principles, not by emotions. I'm going to keep walking by faith. I'm going to finish my race the right way. Nothing is going to knock me off course. I'm going to get back in the fight. I'm going to burn the white flag!"

The Bible tells us that God wants us to be men and women of grit. We will face pressures to quit, to be mediocre, to give in to apathy—but we don't have to give in to the pressure. We don't have to wave the white flag. But it will take grit. Grit is something we can develop. It's something we can teach our kids. We can choose to have more grit, more perseverance, more doggedness. No one is born with grit—it's something we develop in the face of adversity. It's something we choose to build into our value systems, our reactions, our decisions, and our self-identity.

OBSTACLES OF GRIT

A lifestyle of grit is one that takes time and hard work. The opposite of a lifestyle of grit is a lifestyle of apathy. Apathy carries the weight of indifference and passivity. As believers, we cannot give in to apathy as it will make us indifferent to our purpose and unable to carry out the plan God has for our lives. Apathy says, "the obstacles are too big. I will just stay where I am," while grit says, "I can overcome these obstacles and forge my own path."

Some of the obstacles that get in our way and tempt us to live a lifestyle of apathy are self-pity, cowardice, and inconsistency of emotions. These things whisper to us and tell us to stay where we are; they tell us that we can't overcome them. What if we were to listen to *self-pity*? How would that work out as a core value? It wouldn't! Nothing productive comes from self-pity. It saps our energy and our faith. I don't want that for myself, and I don't want to raise children or grandchildren who are always whining and crying and feeling sorry for themselves. There's just no future in self-pity. We overcome self-pity with grit; we speak truth to ourselves to replace the narrative of self-pity.

What if we choose to listen to *cowardice*? That's even worse than self-pity. It's a terrible way to approach life. If we turn and run every time we face something difficult or frightening, we'll never get anywhere. We all know life has scary moments. The question isn't *if* we will face hard times, but *how* we will face them.

What if we choose to give in to *inconsistency*? Yet again, not a great way to live. One day we're feeling fired up, the next day we're dispassionate. One moment we're ready to conquer giants, the next moment we're sure we're going to die. We all have a myriad of emotions that we experience on any given day, but we have to challenge ourselves to not listen to every emotion we experience. We must have the grit to bring our emotions to God and weigh them against His truth.

It almost goes without saying that self-pity, cowardice, and inconsistency don't make for an abundant life. These traits are symptoms of surrendering, and they have no place in our lives. Most people would never consciously choose or identify with those values. But if we don't actively choose grit, we're going to end up falling into one of those things by default. And that's my point. *Get grit.* Decide you are a gritty, persevering, fight-till-you-win kind of person. Then, when troubles and obstacles come, you won't have to think about how you'll respond because you will have burned the white flag long ago.

Not only will you have chosen grit for yourself, but you'll have lived it out for all to see. You will have modeled it for your spouse, your kids, your friends, your coworkers, your employees, and your friends. Because of that, you'll be the person people seek out when they need encouragement. Winners become role models. Everyone wants a winner in their life.

Those same people will hold you accountable when you feel weak. If you make it known that you are a person who stays the course, and if you surround yourself with people who share that value, they are not going to let you quit. Maybe you've seen images of soldiers helping wounded comrades to safety or runners carrying injured competitors over the finish line. We all need friends like that, but it starts with deciding to be a finisher. Grit attracts grit. Strong people attract strong friends. The Bible says, "Iron sharpens iron, and one man sharpens another" (Proverbs 27:17). That's not talking about being abrasive—it's talking about being strong for one another and bringing out the best in one another. We need to be the kind of people who are known for our strength—for being iron for our friends.

GRIT OVER GIFT

I've been reading about Navy SEALs and Special Ops soldiers for years. There's something fascinating to me about people who not only join the military, but sign up for the most grueling, dangerous assignments the military has to offer. These are the cream of the crop, the best of the best. They go out of their way to put themselves in harm's way. That mentality and dedication is inspiring to me.

I read a book called *Extreme Ownership* by Jocko Willink and Leif Babin, former Navy SEALs who now run a leadership training company. They say that when a new batch of recruits would show up for training, everyone else would think they could tell who was going to last. Some people simply looked like SEALs, and some didn't look like they would last a week. But then a few weeks later, they were always amazed at who had quit and who was still there.

They say it's not always the guys who look like they will make it that make it. It's the guys with the most grit. It's the guys who are the most dogged. Often, the most talented guys quit. Why? Because up to that point in their lives, they have been able to get by on talent or gifting. But talent doesn't always get you where you want to go. You need determination, perseverance, and passion.

Potential is one thing, what we do with it is completely different. Some time ago, I read a book by Angela Duckworth titled, *GRIT: The Power of Passion and Perseverance*. She said that she believes that grit is more important than talent. I made a note to myself, "Perseverance or grit matters more in my life than talent or gifting." Yes, we'll be weary at times. But weariness doesn't have to get down into our souls. It doesn't have to make us quit.

Many people have asked me if I've ever thought about quitting.

I remember replying to one man, "Yes, I have."

"What did you do?" he asked.

"I didn't quit."

I think he expected something more profound, but that was all I had. And really, that's what matters most.

I don't think we can help but think about quitting from time to time because we live in a world where that attitude is in the air all the time. Often, it's the first advice you hear from other people: "Just quit." But quitting isn't a solution. It's an escape, and that's not the same thing as a solution.

VOCABULARY OF AN APATHETIC HEART

In the book I read about Navy SEALs, one of the things the authors state is that in life and in leadership, "It's not what you preach, it's what you tolerate."[4] It's one thing to talk a good fight, but what are you actually willing to put up with? What are you settling for? What are you willing to fight to change? This says more about your heart than you realize.

If you've given up, it will come out in your words and actions. Here are a few phrases that might indicate an apathetic heart:

- *That's good enough.* You used to want more or demand more, but something has changed. What didn't use to be good enough is now good enough. Maybe you're listening to the voice of apathy. Don't settle for "good enough" when God wants the best for you.
- *I just don't care anymore.* You used to care. What changed? Often this is a sign you're taking the path of least resistance. Values shouldn't change easily. What was important once is probably still important, deep down—but apathy has told you it's never going to happen, and it wants you to

stop caring. "It used to matter to me that my wife was happy, but I don't care anymore." "I used to care about a good reputation at work, but it's just not that important anymore." That sounds like apathy.

- *It's not worth the effort.* Do you really believe that? You used to think it was. You dreamed, prayed, and worked for it. What changed? Are you just trying to avoid potential disappointment if you try your hardest and fail? Are you weary and looking for a way out?
- *Who cares?* You might say that, but I suspect *you* still care. And your family still cares. And probably a few other people do too. Don't let apathy make you a cynic.
- *Whatever*. It's not too hard to hear the cynicism and defeat in that one. Apathy, discouragement, and doubt have crept in.
- *I'm just going to quit.* We've all felt that way, but that doesn't mean quitting is the only option. That is the voice of apathy speaking.

All these statements could be summarized the same way: "It used to be important to me. I used to believe for it and work for it." If you learn to recognize that tone and that attitude for what it is—apathy—you'll be far better equipped to fight it.

GRIT DON'T QUIT

I have learned, in my forty-plus years of serving God and

living in His kingdom, that there are recurring pressures and voices that try to convince me to wave the white flag. That is to be expected, because the values of God's kingdom are not the values of this world. Before receiving Jesus into my life, I lived in the kingdom of darkness, just like every human ever born. I was part of the world that surrounds us—a world that is often contrary to God's way of thinking. But when I put my faith in Jesus, He transferred me into His kingdom. Colossians 1:13-14 says, "For he has rescued us from the kingdom of darkness and transferred us into the Kingdom of his dear Son, who purchased our freedom and forgave our sins" (NLT).

Now, all of us who have put our faith in Jesus "live and move and have our being" in Jesus and His kingdom (Acts 17:28). For the rest of our lives, we are to grow in understanding about how that kingdom operates, and we are to learn how to align our lives—our spirit, soul, body, finances, relationships, and everything else—with the principles of the kingdom of God.

There are certain inviolable truths that cause this kingdom to operate, and we must live in harmony with them. When we try to live God's way, we often face opposition. Sometimes it's internal, in our hearts, minds, and bodies. Other times it is external, from people and circumstances around us. We face a recurring pressure to give up on the Christian life; to give up on living by faith; to give up on giving; to give up on being His disciples; to give up on being the light of the world and the salt of the earth; to give up on forgiveness; to give up on renewing our minds; to give up on having the right heart attitudes; to give up on believing in the Lord; to give up on believing in His Word; to give up on our dedication to the Lord. It's the temptation to wave the white flag; to surrender to apathy. To go back to how we used to live. To negotiate a ceasefire with the enemy at the cost of our freedom in Christ and our obedience to Him.

I would say the majority of us—probably all of us—have experienced this lure of apathy. It's not every day, and it's not all day long. But it's recurring; it comes back. And sometimes it feels relentless and overpowering. Every time I've stood up to the pressure and pushed back on those thoughts and temptations, they have gone away, and I came out on the other side. I usually think, *Oh, I beat that for good. It's never coming back. I'm never going to feel that way again.* But sooner or later, the voices come around again, trying to get me, my family, or our church to wave the white flag.

The resistance isn't just in our relationship to God. Often it's in relationship to other people or to the abundant life God wants us to experience. Maybe you have had thoughts like this:

- *You might as well give up on going to college.*
- *You might as well give up on putting your kids in a better school.*
- *You might as well give up on finding peace of mind.*
- *You might as well give up on meeting the right person.*
- *You might as well give up on ever being forgiven or ever forgiving.*
- *You might as well give up on achieving financial freedom.*

Or maybe it's even more personal than that.

- *I fail at everything I try. I'll never be enough.*
- *Our family never amounts to anything. Nothing good could happen to me or my family.*
- *My life is a waste. My life should just end.*

Your fight might be mustering the grit to control your temper, changing the words you speak, taking care of yourself physically, building a business, saving your marriage, praying for a child who is not following God, restoring a broken relationship with a friend, beating an addiction, or any other number of things. Maybe you've tried once, twice, or many times to win the fight, but you still struggle from time to time. It can be a bit discouraging when you feel like you beat something and then, a few months or years later, it comes back. I've had people tell me maybe they aren't spiritual enough or disciplined enough. They feel condemned because they find themselves wrestling with something they thought they beat long before. But just because you have to fight something for a few rounds doesn't mean you are less of a winner. I think it makes you more of a winner.

In my experience, it does get easier. Each time you beat something, the victory tends to come a little quicker. The gaps between struggles are a bit longer. The most important thing is to not give up. If you do take some steps backward, don't give in to the temptation to give up completely. Pick yourself up and get back in the fight.

I've thought about quitting. Many times. Let me help you with something, though. There's nothing wrong with thinking about quitting, as long as you don't quit! I've wanted to give up. I've wished I could give up. There have been times I thought I would be forced to quit, whether I wanted to or not. But I never quit. Do you know why? Because I'm not a quitter. Do you know why I'm not a quitter? Because I am a child of God and I have grit. And grit don't quit. It really is that simple. We serve God, and God wins. We know how the Bible ends: with Jesus conquering the world, the flesh, and the devil. That's the side we are on. We might have weak moments, but that will only cause us to pray always, to seek God humbly, and to guard our faith diligently. We won't turn coward. We won't lose our courage. We won't be slothful in our duty. We won't grow weary in hearts or souls. Let's hold onto that conviction throughout our lives. No matter what comes, no matter what emotions or thoughts assault us, we can stand firm.

Fighting against apathy in our daily lives requires grit. Grit to continue praying even when you feel like giving up, grit to listen to who God says you are in the face of what other people are saying about you and the lies you believe about yourself, and grit to seek out friends who will be there for you in every battle you face. Putting on the full armor of God takes grit. Do you have it?

THREE

IGNORE THE ROAR

FIGHT TEMPTATION WITH TRUTH

As we fight for the prize and strive toward the abundant life God has for us, our enemy, the devil, is actively tempting us to stop running toward the prize. The apostle Peter wrote, "Be sober-minded; be watchful. Your adversary the devil prowls around like a roaring lion, seeking someone to devour. Resist him, firm in your faith, knowing that the same kinds of suffering are being experienced by your brotherhood throughout the world" (1 Peter 5:8-9). In other words, our adversary is on the prowl. He's not just looking for a weak person, either: he'll settle for a strong person going through a weak moment. He's on the hunt. He's looking for someone he can frighten with his roar.

I wonder, has the devil been roaring at you? If he has, you're not alone. I would encourage you to keep reading, because I believe even greater faith is coming into your life. You are not going to be afraid of the roaring lion! And you're not going to surrender to his threats and temptations.

Temptations, tests, and trials are not fun. I wish they weren't a part of life. They won't be a part of heaven, which is encouraging to me; but while we're on this planet, they are all too common. They try to get us to surrender, to collapse under the pressure. It is possible to say no to temptation, of course. Just because you're tempted doesn't mean you have to do it. That's not a popular thought in culture today, because a lot of people think they should be allowed to do whatever they want, whenever they want, and however they want. That is not what the abundant life looks like though. Aligning your life with truth means saying no to temptations, but it results in a life that is full and leaves a lasting legacy.

In Luke 4, we read the story of Jesus being tempted by Satan. Jesus spent forty days in the desert, and during that time the devil tried multiple tactics to get Him to wave the white flag of surrender.

Satan started out by saying, "If you're the Son of God" (Luke 4:3). In the original Greek wording, that's a rhetorical *if*. He's not asking a question; he's stating a fact. A more accurate translation is, "*Since* you are the Son of God." In other words, Satan knew who he was dealing with. There was no doubt in his mind who Jesus was. Satan chose to attack Jesus, and he did it when He was going through a physically, mentally, and emotionally challenging period.

This tells us a couple of things about temptations. First, if Satan tempted Jesus, it makes sense that we will face similar temptations. We shouldn't expect smooth sailing all the time any more than Jesus did. Second, experiencing temptation is not an indication of sin or lack of spirituality, because Jesus Himself experienced temptation, and He is perfect. Sometimes the devil tempts us to fail, and then, before we've even failed, he starts to torment us because we're having thoughts of failing. Talk about unfair! The devil fights dirty. Don't let his accusations and condemnation get you down. Just like Jesus resisted, you can resist.

Notice the nature of these temptations. There is a lot we can learn from this. Satan said, "If [since] you are the Son of God, command this stone to become bread" (Luke 4:3).

Jesus replied, "It is written, 'Man shall not live by bread alone'" (verse 4).

So, the devil changed tactics. He took Him up to the top of a high mountain. Luke says the devil showed Jesus "all the kingdoms of the world in a moment of time" (verse 5). Then he told Jesus, "To you I will give all this authority and their glory, for it has been delivered to me, and I give it to whom I will. If you, then, will worship me, it will all be yours" (verses 6-7). I love Jesus' reply. He didn't give in for a second. He said, "It is written, 'You shall worship the Lord your God, and Him only shall you serve'" (verse 8).

The devil tried one last time. He took Jesus to Jerusalem, to the pinnacle of the temple, and said, "If you are the Son of God, throw yourself down from here." Then he had the nerve to quote the Bible to Jesus. He referred to Psalm 91: "For it is written, 'He will command his angels concerning you, to guard you,' and 'On their hands they will bear you up, lest you strike your foot against a stone'" (verses 9-11). Jesus quoted the Bible right back at him, "It is said, 'You shall not put the Lord your God to the test'" (verse 12).

The story ends with the devil defeated, but only for a season. "And when the devil had ended every temptation, he departed from him until an opportune time" (verse 13). Not forever. He came back. You can see Satan's efforts in the rest of the gospels in the form of persecution, lies, accusations, threats, plots against Jesus' life, Judas' betrayal, and eventually the crucifixion itself.

Notice that these temptations centered on three areas:

- Satan tried to get Jesus to depend on His own resources: "Command this stone to become bread." This was a temptation to live independently of God.
- He tried to get Jesus to force the hand of God. "Throw yourself down." This was a temptation to force God to make up for our pride and foolishness.
- He tried to get Jesus to refuse Cavalry. "If you, then, will worship me, it will all be yours." In other words, "You don't have to go to Cavalry. You don't have to go to the cross." Remember, Satan always wanted to be like the Most High. Isn't that interesting? So, he tried to get the Most High to bow down and worship him, because he wanted to be like God (Isaiah 14:14). This was a temptation to sidestep God's plan.

God had a glorious plan for Jesus' life; it was a plan that required pain and sacrifice, but it resulted in the fullness of joy for God, Jesus, and all of us. Satan tempted Jesus to pursue a path that would require less sacrifice, a plan that would ultimately be unsatisfying. Satan tempts us in the same ways every day. He tempts us to follow paths that will not lead to the abundant life God has for us.

Satan tempts us to live independently of God. God, through His Word, has given us guidelines to live by so we might experience the fullness of joy in His presence during our time on earth. When we ignore those guidelines and follow the unchecked desires of our hearts, we tend to follow paths that won't lead to prosperity. Living independently of God means not going to Him with our needs, our desires, and our requests. One way we are tempted to live independently of God is through lust. When we hear the word *lust*, we often think of sexual desire. But that is an incomplete understanding for two reasons. First, sexual desire in and of itself is not wrong; God created sex, and He meant for it to be enjoyed within the context of the marriage covenant. Second, lust can include far more than just misplaced sexual passion. Lust is *an inordinate desire* or *a desire that has gone to a place where it shouldn't be*. You might desire success, and that desire is godly; but that desire can become a lust when it grows out of proportion and begins to destroy your life. Similarly, you can desire more money, and that desire isn't necessarily wrong. Rather, it is the *lust* for money that is the root of all kinds of evil (1 Timothy 6:10).

We all have desires, but if we are not careful, Satan will take those desires and blow them up to levels where they shouldn't be. They will become overpowering forces that cause us to want things and pursue things we shouldn't. Satan wants us to surrender to those lusts, but the good news is that we don't have to. He can't make us. "The devil made me do it" is a cop-out, because the devil doesn't have that kind of power or control. In Jesus, we are free to make up our own minds and choose our own paths.

What is going on in your life, your finances, and your mind right now? Are there pressures being applied to you to give in to your lusts? If so, burn the white flag! You don't have to give in or give up. Declare to yourself and the devil, "I'm not going to surrender to that!"

Romans 12 refers to these desires as the "fleeting fashions of the world."[5] That's not talking about your style choices or the clothes you wear, but about the thoughts you think. *I know the Bible says this, but everybody else thinks that. Everybody else is doing that. Maybe the Bible is out of date. Maybe the Word of God doesn't apply anymore.* I'm not picking on anyone here but the devil. I'm pulling back the shroud of darkness he uses to deceive us and fool us into thinking we should conform to the world and live independently of God instead of being conformed to the image of God's dear Son and living in unity with Him. The way to fight against this temptation to live independently of God is to speak truth to the temptations, as Jesus did.

Satan tempts us to make foolish choices and think we can force God to cover for our arrogance. "Throw yourself down," Satan says. Nowhere did God even hint to that kind of foolishness. Yet, so often, we are tempted to do something similar. I remember a man telling me he could commit adultery because God was obligated to forgive him. And how many times have I heard of people spending money they did not have, thinking they could force God to catch them, as Satan suggested to Jesus. Paul writes in 1 Corinthians 10:23, "'I have the right to do anything,' you say—but not everything is beneficial. 'I have the right to do anything'—but not everything is constructive" (NIV). Jesus modeled that for us. Acting foolish because you know that "no matter what, God will forgive you" is not using the freedom and grace that God offers in a beneficial way. Fight against these temptations by asking yourself, "Is what I'm about to do beneficial to me and the people around me?"

Satan tempts us to try to sidestep God's plan for our lives. This temptation grows out of us thinking we know what is best for us; we think we know better than the God who created us! Numbers 20 tells a story about the Israelites wandering in the desert after leaving Egypt, and they need water. Their leader, Moses, makes this known to God. And God says to Moses, "Take the staff, and assemble the congregation, you and Aaron your brother, and tell the rock before their eyes to yield its water. So you shall bring water out of the rock for them and give drink to the congregation . . ." (Numbers 20:8). All Moses has to do is speak to a rock . . . easy. Moses gathers the Israelites together, "'Hear now, you rebels: shall we bring water for you out of this rock?' And Moses lifted up his hand and struck the rock with his staff twice, and water came out abundantly, and the congregation drank, and their livestock" (verses 10-12). Moses went rogue; he didn't talk to the rock, instead he hit it with the staff. Moses didn't follow God's instructions because he thought he knew better. God still provided water for the Israelites, but Moses did have to suffer the consequences of sidestepping God's plan, "And the Lord said to Moses and Aaron, 'Because you did not believe in me, to uphold me as holy in the eyes of the people of Israel, therefore you shall not bring this assembly into the land that I have given them'" (verse 13). Because Moses sidestepped God's plan, he was unable to go into the Promised Land. We must resist the temptation to sidestep God's instructions, always remembering that God knows what is best for us.

In moments of weariness, weakness, and desperation, the temptation is to bypass God and do things ourselves. It is to try to manipulate God into doing what we want. And it is to find a shortcut around God's will that avoids difficulty. When we face these temptations, we must look to Jesus, the ultimate example for how to handle these temptations. Jesus spoke truth in the face of temptations; He didn't surrender, He fought back with truth.

FOUR

UNDER PRESSURE

FIGHT WEARINESS WITH JOY

Both General George Patton and renowned football coach Vince Lombardi are quoted as saying, "Fatigue makes cowards of us all."[6] I'm guessing they both said that because it's as applicable to soldiers as it is to athletes—and it is applicable to us as well. Weariness has a way of affecting our decisions, words, and actions without us realizing it.

Now, I feel weary every time the alarm clock goes off, but that's not the kind of weariness we're talking about here. This is a weariness of the soul. It might include physical tiredness, but it goes far beyond that. The Greek word for *weary* means *faint-hearted, weak, feeble, to have it badly, to grow impatient or dissatisfied, to crumble, to break down*. The pressures we face have the potential, over time, to bring us to a place of faint-heartedness and weakness. They will get us to crumble and break down. They will make us focus on how bad our situation is. We all think we have it bad at times or that we don't have the strength to continue. That's the point of this passage, though. Jesus made it through, and so can we. We can't let weariness win, and we can't faint under pressure.

Hebrews 12:3 says, "Think of him [Jesus] who endured such opposition against himself by sinners, so that you may not grow weary in your souls and give up" (NET). The phrase "grow weary" is very important here. The author of Hebrews essentially says that weariness left unchecked will result in surrender. After telling us about all the heroes of faith through the ages, and after telling us to run with endurance, the author of Hebrews gives us a helpful insight into running the race well, "looking to Jesus, the founder and perfecter of our faith, who for the joy that was set before him endured the cross, despising the shame, and is seated at the right hand of the throne of God" (Hebrews 12:2). Notice why Jesus was able to endure the cross: "for the joy that was set before him." Many centuries earlier, one of the leaders of Israel, a man named Nehemiah, shared a similar sentiment, "the joy of the Lord is your strength" (Nehemiah 8:10). Joy brings us strength. Not just any joy—the joy that comes from knowing and following God. The joy that comes from God Himself when we place our trust in Him. You know you are truly trusting God when you are able to have joy even in tough circumstances and believe for God to give you joy!

That's not normal, by the way. And people will even question you, "Why are you so happy? Why are you so optimistic? Don't you see what happening? Don't you care?"

Of course we know what's going on. But we also know that the circumstances around us are not the sum of our reality. Just as Jesus was with Peter and the disciples in the storm, so He is with us. That awareness allows the joy and peace of God to flourish even when we face adversity.

JOY ROBBERS

Right after I turned forty, I ruptured a disc in my back. The pain was extreme, but I didn't know I had ruptured a disc because I didn't go to the doctor. Like a typical male, I figured it would go away if I ignored it.

It didn't. I suffered for nearly a year. One night, the discomfort was so bad I couldn't sleep, so I got up and went into the kitchen. At that point, my body was so weary from pain that I fainted. I woke up a few minutes later on the floor, and I had to crawl back to bed.

On the positive side, fainting made me realize I couldn't keep ignoring the underlying cause. I needed to go see an orthopedic surgeon. After he finished scolding me for waiting so long, he scheduled surgery. He repaired the rupture, and I've been healthy ever since.

Fainting was an indication that something was wrong with my body and needed to be fixed before I did irreparable damage. The same goes with our souls. Faintness of heart is a sign that something is wrong on the inside: with our thoughts, our emotions, our spirits, our souls, our motivations, our values, our focus. When you are weary, it is easy to put comfort before joy. When we are weary, it is easy for us to not press in to God and to community. Here are a few things I've observed that can cause weariness and faintness and try to rob you of joy.

Loneliness can cause weariness.

Living a different lifestyle than the world and having different priorities than the world can be really lonely at times. Jesus understood this well. Earlier in this chapter, we looked at how Jesus endured the cross, despising the shame associated with a criminal's death. The author of Hebrews says Jesus is our example of endurance, and, as we look to Him, we can also run our race with endurance. But Jesus didn't just face shame and ridicule. He also faced outright opposition. Bad people with bad intentions attempted to take Him down, and ultimately they succeeded—or at least, they thought they did.

Jesus' critics didn't get what He was trying to do. For that matter, His friends didn't always get what He was trying to do. A lot of times, people won't understand you. They won't understand what kind of marriage you're trying to build. They won't understand what kind of kids you're trying to raise. They won't understand why your priorities have changed since you became a Christian or started going to church. They won't understand why you give money away, why you forgive offenses, why you refuse to gossip, why you give your time and energy to help people and build the church, why you're honest in your business dealings, or why you pay your taxes fairly. But you do. You know the race you're running and the prize you're after, and you know Jesus is waiting for you at the end. You know it's worth it, so don't listen to the peanut gallery.

If you've read the gospels or heard much teaching about Jesus' life, then you've probably seen this hostility and opposition in operation through the Pharisees, the scribes, and the Sadducees. They were constantly contradicting Him and constantly trying to shame Him. They called Him names: heretic, insane, liar, false prophet, demon-possessed. They tried to trap, dismiss, or intimidate Him. They insinuated He was conceived from adultery. They attempted to discredit Him with the people. Ultimately, they accused Him of crimes He never committed and had Him arrested.

If Jesus endured both shame and opposition, it stands to reason that we will too. Hebrews 12:3 says as much. "Consider him who endured from sinners such hostility against himself, so that you may not grow weary or fainthearted." We face similar loneliness today. People don't understand us or what we stand for. Maybe you've faced hostility too. You are just trying to live your life according to the Word of God. You are just trying to love people, do good, and be at peace. Yet there are people around you who make fun of you. They label you, criticize you, and mock you. Why? For the same reason they did it to Jesus. Satan is trying to get you to say, "I can't take this. This hurts too much." He wants you to lose courage and faint.

Hostility is not a nice word. Most of us try to avoid hostile situations and hostile people. But sometimes our decision to run our race with courage and conviction will incite resistance in others. You wouldn't think so. Why should it bother people if you want to choose to follow God, love your neighbor, and in general, live well? I think some people don't react well to being reminded that they are not living the way God intended them to, and if they can hold us back, subconsciously it will make them feel better about themselves. The apostle Peter, referring to people who don't understand why we live the way we do, said this: "Of course, your former friends are surprised when you no longer plunge into the flood of wild and destructive things they do. So they slander you" (1 Peter 4:4 NLT).

I've had people do this to me and to our church over the years. They came with the intention of finding fault so they could embarrass us. It's not for me to judge their motivations, but I can tell you that it wasn't easy for me emotionally to deal with the slander and hostility. I think most of us like to be liked. So, when people come against us, it can be tempting to compromise our actions or values to avoid being the target. That's not what Jesus did though. He endured rejection and endured hostility.

Years ago, there was a preacher in El Paso who decided he didn't like me, he didn't like our church, and he didn't like what we were doing. I really don't know what the issue was, because we never had a conflict. He had a radio program, and every day he would say evil things about me and call me names on the program. It got really ugly, actually. Maybe he assumed I'd never find out, but of course people come and tell you when they hear things like that.

Somebody asked me one day, "Pastor, aren't you concerned about what this man thinks about you?"

I said, "You know what? I'm really not."

"Really? You don't care?"

I had never thought of this before, but it just came out of my spirit. I said, "No, because at the end of my life, he's not going to be the one waiting for me."

The one I am going to meet at the end of my life is the Lord Jesus. And I want Him to say, "Well done, good and faithful servant." It doesn't matter what that pastor thought or said. What matters is what Jesus thinks about me. And that thought—fixing my thoughts on Jesus—replaced my feelings of weariness, loneliness, and being misunderstood with joy.

So what should you do when you feel lonely? Hebrews 12:2 gave us the answer, and we looked at it earlier. When you become weary as you live differently than the world, turn your eyes to Jesus. He persevered, and you can too. Think about the race before you. Think of the joy set before you. Think about the prize ahead. Think about the One who is waiting for you at the end of the race: Jesus Himself. Imagine Him saying, "Well done, good and faithful servant."

Sorrow can cause weariness.

Sometimes the weariness we face is found within our own hearts and emotions. Specifically, *sorrow* can cause us to become weary. The prophet Jeremiah connected the two when he said, "I would comfort myself in sorrow; my heart is faint in me" (Jeremiah 8:18 NKJV). All of us go through sorrow—it's a real, human emotion—but you must set a limit on sorrow. I've learned about sorrow. I swam in that ocean. You beat yourself up with it because you think you should have been better or you could have done better. Even though you did well, there are always things you could have done better.

Many years ago, my best friend took his own life. It shattered me. I couldn't speak his name without crying for probably three years after. I thought about what I could have said, or how I could have helped, or how I wished I had more time with him. The sorrow I felt robbed me of joy for a long time.

But recently, I was called in for jury duty, and, during the hours of waiting, I began a conversation with a gentleman on the jury. His son had also taken his own life, less than two months before, and I could see his sorrow. We spent the entire day together, and I listened as he poured out his heart, asking me questions and searching for answers. I was refreshed by the connection that I felt with him. Sorrow causes weariness when we carry it alone, but when we open up and carry sorrow with others, it creates connection and a deep, unmatched joy.

Sorrow is real, and there is a time for it. Ecclesiastes says there is "a time to weep, and a time to laugh; a time to mourn, and a time to dance" (Ecclesiastes 3:4). Some sorrow can be good, but you need to be careful with it. At some point, you have to climb out of that ocean. At some point, you've got to stop looking inward and look up. Look for people who can help you carry your grief.

Tap into the joy of the Lord which is your strength (Nehemiah 8:10), because sorrow can cause your heart to faint. It can cause you to start thinking you can never be happy again. You were happy, but now you can't be happy. You start to lose faith, lose heart, lose courage. You have to watch out for that mindset. It will creep into your thoughts and emotions, and it will cause you great weariness. Learn to lean upon God, even in sorrow, and to find strength and joy in Him.

Comparison can cause weariness.

The apostle Paul wrote, "Do not be deceived: God is not mocked, for whatever one sows, that will he also reap" (Galatians 6:7). That phrase "Do not be deceived" is there for good reason: sometimes we think we know better than God, but we don't. God's ways always work in the end. Just because our immediate circumstances don't make sense to us doesn't mean God's eternal principles suddenly stopped working. Just because someone else seems to be reaping benefits without following God's ways doesn't mean they've found a shortcut. Just because someone seems to be living the Christian walk better than you, or they seem holier than you and seem to have their life together, doesn't mean you should give up. You must fight against comparison; comparison causes weariness and drains your joy.

God is not mocked. In other words, no one is smarter than Him. His principles work, His ways are perfect, and His rewards will come in due time. Sooner or later, God is proved true. Our problem is that we can usually handle the sooner, but we don't have the patience to wait for the later. We look at other people and want their lives without appreciating the path and plan God has called us to.

Galatians 6:8 says, "For the one who sows to his own flesh will from the flesh reap corruption, but the one who sows to the Spirit will from the Spirit reap eternal life." There are two kinds of seed: flesh and Spirit. The flesh compares; the Spirit rejoices. The flesh seeks to follow the path of someone else; the Spirit follows God's path for us. Keep sowing the right kind of seed. Keep doing the right thing.

Verse 9 continues, "And let us not grow weary of doing good, for in due season we will reap, if we do not give up." Notice that word *weary*, which we've looked at in other passages. Paul is saying that in our sowing and living, we can't become faint-hearted. We can't start focusing on how bad life is. Just keep doing good. Keep sowing good seed. Keep thinking the right way. Keep believing the right things. Keep going in the right direction. Don't sow to the flesh. Don't be led astray. Don't be pulled off track. Don't wave the white flag and surrender to the world.

DON'T MAKE ME CROSS OVER

When we give in to loneliness, sorrow, and comparison, and let them rob us of our joy and make us weary, we are likely to forfeit the abundant life that God has for us. The Israelites are an example of this. After the Israelites had wandered in the desert for a while because they refused to enter the Promised Land, they had another chance. The children who had watched their parents give up in discouragement had all grown up, and they had learned their lesson. They were ready to enter the Promised Land.

Well, most of them were ready. As Israel was preparing to finally cross the Jordan River and march into the land, two of the twelve tribes came to Moses. They said they were comfortable where they were at. There was enough land and pasture for their livestock. They asked, "Let this land be given to your servants as our possession.

Do not make us cross the Jordan" (Numbers 32:5 NIV).

Moses got mad. He was really steamed up. He said, "Should your fellow Israelites go to war while you sit here? Why do you discourage the Israelites from crossing over into the land the Lord has given them? This is what your fathers did . . ." (verses 6-8 NIV). Then he called them a "brood of sinners" (verse 14 NIV) and used a few other colorful phrases.

Moses realized two things. First, these two tribes were giving in to the temptation to settle for less than the best. Second, they could easily discourage the hearts of their fellow Israelites.

The two tribes assured Moses they would fight alongside their brothers until the land was conquered, and, to their credit, they did exactly that later in the story. But they never asked for an inheritance in the land. They built their homes and established their lives on the other side of the Jordan, just shy of God's promise.

The ways these tribes expressed themselves says a lot about their weariness. They were comfortable and they didn't want to be bothered. How dare anyone make them move? How dare anyone challenge their comfortable lifestyle? It is amazing to me how many people see from a distance the abundant life Jesus wants them to have and decide they don't want it. They don't want to live terrible lives, of course, so they make a few changes; but once their lives are more or less put together, they get comfortable. They don't want to put in the discipline and work to attain all God wants to give them.

God didn't force these two tribes to move. He didn't force the prior generation to enter the land. And He won't force you or me, either. He tells us how great the future is, and He promises to give it to us, but only if we want it. Only if we are willing to possess it. But only in taking hold of God's promises can we fight weariness and receive the fullness of joy.

In the face of weariness, then, how do you fight? How do you stop fainting and start fighting? Isaiah 40:31 is one of my all-time favorite verses when I'm feeling a bit burned out; it has brought me through so much fire and pressure over the years, "They who wait for the Lord shall renew their strength; they shall mount up with wings like eagles; they shall run and not be weary; they shall walk and not faint."

What does waiting for the Lord mean? I can tell you what it *doesn't* mean. It doesn't mean saying a quick prayer and then living your life as if God weren't involved. Waiting is not about doing nothing, but rather about actively seeking and trusting God to do what only He can do. In the original Hebrew text, *They who wait for the Lord* means *they who gather together before the Lord.* Do you know where that happens best? Do you know where you can connect with God, experience the support of others, and hear God's Word spoken to your situation? *In church.* Church is one of God's greatest strategies to help us stay strong in difficult times. And I don't believe that because I'm a pastor—I'm a pastor because I believe that. I've seen the power of living life with a community of like-minded, spiritually-engaged people. Deep, meaningful relationships help heal the weariness that comes from loneliness, sorrow, and comparison.

I'm not saying the church is perfect—clearly it's not.

It's made up of imperfect people, so there will be issues and challenges from time to time. But when you position yourself in an atmosphere of faith, Scripture, worship, and prayer, you'll find the joy and strength you need.

Most importantly of all, when you gather with other believers, Jesus is there. He said where two or three gather together in His name, He will be there with them (Matthew 18:20). Don't fight your battles alone. When you face pressure to quit, that is all the more reason to strengthen your connection to God and His church.

Many times I've walked into church exhausted and walked out rejuvenated. I can't explain it. You'd think it would be the opposite, but many people have told me the same thing. They come in feeling tired, discouraged, and mentally and physically fatigued; and then something happens. They spend time worshiping. They hear the Word, and faith arises in their hearts. They spend a few minutes talking with other people. And they walk out completely different.

When you feel pressured to faint—to get wearied—don't stay away from church. Run to it! Go more, not less. Why? Because when you draw close to God, when you wait on Him and for Him, He will renew your strength. He will cause you to mount up on wings like eagles. You will run and not be weary; you will walk and not faint.

FIVE

OVERCOMING SHADOWS

FIGHT DECEPTION WITH PERSPECTIVE

A few years ago, as I was returning home after work, I pulled up to my driveway and noticed something odd. My garage sits on the side of the house, and as I was pulling in, I saw somebody moving inside my house, behind my front doors. I put my car in reverse, backed out of the driveway, and frantically called 911.

The operator asked, "What's your emergency?"

"I was pulling into my driveway, and I saw somebody in my house."

"Sir, please don't go in."

"Don't worry. I'm not planning on it."

She took my name and address and said she'd send someone to check it out. I sat there in my car, waiting for help, and thoughts started going through my head. *Where are the security guys when you need them? . . . I live in a gated community. What good does paying my dues do? . . . Maybe I should get a gun.* Lots of thoughts, mostly dumb ones.

Then suddenly I had another thought, and I decided to test it out. I drove back into the driveway, just as I had before. I realized that at a certain point, the sun hit my car's front windshield just right, which caused a reflection on the front door. Because it's a smoked-glass door, it looked like somebody was moving behind it.

So, I called 911 again. "Excuse me. I just called you a minute ago."

"Yes, sir. Has something happened?"

"Well, not exactly. I just realized there was no one moving in my house. It was the sunlight reflecting off my car and onto the door."

There was silence for a moment. I'm pretty sure it was because the operator had put her hand over the receiver and was laughing out loud.

I said, "Hello? Are you still there?"

She said, "I called the officers and told them they don't need to go to your house unless you really want them to."

"I don't really want them to. I'm actually just very embarrassed. Thank you so much." I got out of the car and went into my house. Naturally, there was no one there.

Here's my point: the figure inside my house was nothing but a shadow, but I perceived it to be real. And my false perception stopped me just as effectively as a real intruder would have. Perceptions take on a life of their own. They seem real to us, and they affect us deeply. We go to the movie theater, and even though we know we're watching a movie, our heart rates go up. We cringe in our seats. Some of you even scream. I've heard you. It's the power of perception. I've heard it said that reality is not what *is*; it's what we *perceive* it to be. It's amazing how much our perceptions affect us.

There was a comedian in the '70s named Flip Wilson. One of his classic lines was, "A lie is as good as the truth as long as you get somebody to believe it." It's true. You can believe a lie, and, for you, that becomes truth. It is quite a thought. That perception determines how you react, how you believe, how you create, and how you treat people.

The word *perception* literally means *a taking in* or *an awareness derived from a stimulus*. My perception is created by what I take in. What my senses receive and how I interpret that information creates my perception of reality.

In the world we live in, we are flooded with information, opinions, stimuli, and data. Our senses are constantly being bombarded, and our minds work overtime to process what we receive. The question becomes, who am I letting influence me, and what am I allowing into my heart? Because that is creating my perception. I need to ask myself:

- Who am I looking to for truth?
- Who am I looking to for inspiration?
- Who am I looking to for guidance?
- Who am I looking to for correction?
- How accurate is my perception of my life, my calling, and my ability?
- How is my perception affecting how I look at the people and the opportunities in my life?

The scariest thing about perception is that we can't really tell if our perception is off—at least not on our own. That's why deception is so dangerous: no one knows when they're deceived. That's the nature of deception and misperception. So are we doomed to deceit? Or is there a way to calibrate our thoughts and our perceptions to a more reliable standard? As a matter of fact, there are a couple ways.

SEEING STRAIGHT

The first and best source of accurate perceptions is the Bible. The Word is alive and full of power, it separates the good from the bad, and it is a discerner of the thoughts and intents of the heart (see Hebrews 4:12). The Word we read and hear has the power to come into our hearts and divide things up for us. It tells us, "You have some perceptions here that are correct, and you have some over here that are wrong. Let's cultivate the correct ones and get rid of the wrong ones so you can have the life God wants you to have."

The words and truths in the Bible are God's wisdom for life on earth. Everything that is in the Word, including the "dos and don'ts," are there to make our lives better. The Bible says His commandments, His instructions, and His wisdom "are not burdensome" (1 John 5:3). God does not give us His Word to make our lives worse, but rather to reveal truth and give us abundant life.

There is a conflict at times between our flesh (which includes our thoughts, desires, and emotions) and the Word. The world often tries to tell us that God doesn't get it—that He is old-fashioned, that society has changed, that we shouldn't think like that anymore. We can reject God's wisdom, but we won't like the long-term result. Everything in the Bible is given to us to let us know how life works best. It's an objective, unchanging source of wisdom, and as we align our perspectives and perceptions to it, we will find peace and success.

No one has all the answers, and isolation is dangerous. We need to continually put ourselves in positions where we can learn from those who are wiser and more experienced than us. We should seek out people we respect who are willing to shoot straight with us. No matter how young or old we are, and no matter how smart or experienced we are, all of us need correction, guidance, inspiration, truth, and information, because none of us are perfect.

The apostle John wrote, "Beloved, I pray that all may go well with you and that you may be in good health, as it goes well with your soul" (3 John 1:2). That is God's desire: that our souls and our lives would be healthy, secure, and fruitful. Listening to God, obeying God, and living according to the Word of God will promote health and prosperity in our lives. Thinking the way He wants us to think and believing the way He wants us to believe will bring good things to our lives. But we have to guard our perspective and our perceptions, because if we aren't careful, we can lose sight of how good God is and end up getting discouraged by the pressures and battles along the way.

EXPECT OPPOSITION

The Bible specifically records how good God had been

to Israel and how many times He had proven Himself to them. God Himself says, speaking of the people who rebelled, that they "have seen my glory and my signs that I did in Egypt and in the wilderness, and yet have put me to the test these ten times and have not obeyed my voice" (Numbers 14:22).

These were people who had seen God's glory and miracles in Egypt and in the wilderness. They had seen the Red Sea open up so they could walk through on dry ground. They had seen water come out of a rock. They had seen bitter water turned into safe drinking water. They had seen snake bites cured. They had seen victory over the enemies that attacked them. They had seen God provide supernatural food every day for them. They had seen how their clothes and sandals didn't wear out. They knew God was on their side, and they knew what God could do. Yet their perception was about to change and rob them of the Promised Land.

When the Promised Land was finally in their grasp, Israel sent twelve spies into the land, and they were gone forty days. When they came back, they gave their report to all of Israel, "We came to the land to which you sent us. It flows with milk and honey, and this is its fruit" (Numbers 13:27). In other words, God had done what He promised. The spies acknowledged that God had brought them to the land, and it was exactly as He had said. It was a land that flowed with milk and honey, a land that promoted health and prosperity.

I'm sure everyone listening was excited and ready to go. But the spies weren't done with their report:

> "However, the people who dwell in the land are strong, and the cities are fortified and very large. And besides, we saw the descendants of Anak there. The Amalekites dwell in the land of the Negeb. The Hittites, the Jebusites, and the Amorites dwell in the hill country. And the Canaanites dwell by the sea, and along the Jordan." (Numbers 13:28-29)

Fear began to rise among the Israelites. Caleb and Joshua were the only spies who saw these obstacles but had faith in the God who brought them to this land:

> But Caleb quieted the people before Moses and said, "Let us go up at once and occupy it, for we are well able to overcome it." Then the men who had gone up with him said, "We are not able to go up against the people, for they are stronger than we are." (Numbers 13:30-31)

We see a fundamental difference in outlook between the encouraged spies and the discouraged spies. Caleb and Joshua said they were able; the rest said they were not able—that they were weaker than the inhabitants. How do they know the enemy was better than them or stronger than them if they had never fought them? They had not gone to battle with any of these people yet, and yet their perception was, "We can't beat them; we can't do what they do; we can't overcome them."

The problem is that their perceptions were *wrong*, therefore, their decisions were wrong. It's one thing to have an accurate estimation of your abilities and a challenge you are facing. The Bible talks about planning, wisdom, and good decisions. But our decisions have to take into account the Word, the power, and the promises of God. That is where Israel went wrong. They looked at themselves, they looked at their enemies, and they gave up before they even started, even though God Himself had promised they could win.

Jesus told us in John 16:33 that in this life we will have tribulations. He warned us we would have temptations, tests, and trials, and He told us we would need to have courage, perseverance, and grit. Opposition is a real part of life, and it shouldn't take us by surprise.

"They're stronger than us," Israel said; and with that, they removed God from their equation. They had seen God's power in similarly impossible situations, but when it came time to conquer the land, they allowed their perception to change.

There are many members of the military in my church, and I learn a lot from them. They've told me there is a famous saying in the armed forces: "The enemy gets a vote." In other words, you can make your plans and form your strategies, but the enemy doesn't have to cooperate. And they probably won't.

The Amalekites, the Jebusites, and the rest of the tribes and nations in the land had a vote. I think that was what scared Israel. They realized they couldn't control everything or guarantee a favorable outcome, and they panicked. But they forgot something. God also has a vote.

You don't hear them say one word about God. All you hear is, "We can't. We're not able. They are stronger. We are weak." Their shortsighted, limited perceptions removed God from the equation. And that stopped them as suddenly and effectively as if their enemies had already beaten them. They were defeated by shadows.

I can tell you from my own experience, it is easy to be strong when you are in a good place in life. But things change so quickly, and suddenly you find yourself thinking, *I have it so bad. This is terrible. There's no hope.* What happened? God is still real, He's still strong, and He's still on your side. Yes, circumstances might have changed, but what really matters is that your perception changed.

CALLING THE BLUFF

The discouraged spies continued their report, now with the addition of a few dramatic details:

> So they brought to the people of Israel a bad report of the land that they had spied out, saying, "The land, through which we have gone to spy it out, is a land that devours its inhabitants, and all the people that we saw in it are of great height." (Numbers 13:32)

They've started contradicting themselves . . . changing their story. Earlier they said the land flowed with milk and honey, which means it was full of health and prosperity, and that everyone in it was strong. Now, they say the land "devours its inhabitants." What does that even mean? Is it a good place or a bad place? Is it a land that creates giants or eats up its inhabitants?

What they were really trying to do here was discourage the people from entering the land. They had allowed deception to discourage them, and now they were spreading it to others. They were saying, "Let's wave the white flag. Let's give up now because otherwise we're going to die fighting."

The conclusion of their report was this: "And there we saw the Nephilim (the sons of Anak, who come from the Nephilim), and we seemed to ourselves like grasshoppers, and so we seemed to them" (verse 33).

How did they know how the inhabitants of the land viewed them? As far we know, they didn't talk to anyone. The people everywhere knew Israel was coming for them, and they were on the lookout. They wanted to capture and kill them, not sit them down for coffee and tell them how cute and grasshoppery they looked. Yet the spies had the audacity to assume they knew what the people were thinking.

The way the spies expressed themselves here is incredibly revealing. Read it again. "We seemed to ourselves like grasshoppers, and so we seemed to them." The first half was true—they clearly had a low opinion of themselves. But who gave them the right to assume the second half? "So we seemed to them." Says who? Did they conduct an opinion poll? Did they interview a cross sample of the giants to reach that conclusion? No! They were simply projecting their own negative perception upon those around them. They saw themselves as small and weak, so they assumed everyone else saw them that way as well.

It didn't matter how the inhabitants of the land saw Israel. What mattered was how Israel saw Israel. It's the same in your life, my friend. What your boss thinks of you, what your mama thinks of you, what your ex thinks of you, or what some blogger thinks of you matters far less than what *you* think of you.

We try to figure out what people think about us, and it just gets weird. Unless they tell us what they think, we simply don't know. So, we end up basing our actions and reactions on our perception of their perception of us, and that's just confusing. The Bible says, "For who knows a person's thoughts except their own spirit within them?" (1 Corinthians 2:11 NIV). In other words, you don't really know what someone else is thinking about you.

The truth is, they might not be thinking about you at all! That's a liberating thought. I used to be driven by what I thought people were thinking about me. It's such a trap. Then I realized that most people weren't thinking about me at all. They are thinking about their own lives and their own needs. They have a lot more to worry about than criticizing or mocking me in their minds. I'm not that important!

The story doesn't get any better. Thanks to their false perceptions, Israel decided they wanted to run away.

> Then all the congregation raised a loud cry, and the people wept that night. And all the people of Israel grumbled against Moses and Aaron. The whole congregation said to them, "Would that we had

> died in the land of Egypt! Or would that we had died in this wilderness! Why is the Lord bringing us into this land, to fall by the sword? Our wives and our little ones will become a prey. Would it not be better for us to go back to Egypt?" And they said to one another, "Let us choose a leader and go back to Egypt." (Numbers 14:1-4)

Go back to Egypt? The lack of logic in this statement goes to show the power of false perceptions. Egypt held nothing for them but slavery and probably death. Fear has a dark power to make captivity seem attractive, to make settling look like luxury, and to make surrender seem easy.

In our lives, what would we go back to? How would quitting help us? Peter wrote this, referring to people who had turned their backs on the truths of Jesus: "The proverbs are true: 'A dog returns to its vomit,' and, 'A sow that is washed returns to her wallowing in the mud'" (2 Peter 2:22 NIV). I'm not a dog or a pig! And I'm not going back.

Don't believe the deceptions of the enemy in your mind—the lies that say you aren't strong enough or big enough. With God on your side, you are not a grasshopper. You are a giant, a conqueror, a champion. The devil is afraid of you, and he'll try to bluff you into giving up. Call his bluff! Call him out on his lies! God is not going to bring you to the edge of His promise only to abandon you at the last second.

GAINING PERSPECTIVE

The discouraged spies were wrong in their evaluation. The inhabitants of the land were terrified of Israel. How do I know that? Because forty years later, when Joshua and the new generation were about to enter the Promised Land, Joshua sent two spies into the land first. These two spies went to Jericho, where they met a woman named Rahab, who protected and hid them. Rahab said this to them:

> I know that the Lord has given you this land and that a great fear of you has fallen on us, so that all who live in this country are melting in fear because of you. We have heard how the Lord dried up the water of the Red Sea for you when you came out of Egypt, and what you did to Sihon and Og, the two kings of the Amorites east of the Jordan, whom you completely destroyed. When we heard of it, our hearts melted in fear and everyone's courage failed because of you, for the Lord your God is God in heaven above and on the earth below. (Joshua 2:9-11 NIV)

That does not sound like grasshopper language at all! And this is forty years after the events she described had taken place. For forty years, the people of the land had lived in fear, knowing a more powerful nation with a more powerful God was coming for them. Apparently, the only ones who didn't get that memo were the Israelites. Rahab says the hearts of everyone in the land were "melting in fear." They were filled with discouragement. They were afraid. They recognized the power of God at work in Israel. Had Israel actually advanced like God wanted them to, many of those nations would have probably waved their white flags in surrender without so much as a fight. But Israel waved theirs first. They had less confidence in the power of God than their enemies did. Israel saw themselves as grasshoppers and the people of the land as giants. But the people in the land saw Israel as the giants.

Shadows can be scary, but they aren't real. Their only power is in their ability to deceive. Don't let threats or fears get into your heart. Don't let a limited, human evaluation of your circumstances take your eyes off Jesus. Don't factor God out of your equation—factor Him in everywhere you can.

There will be opposition. The devil might tell you to give up because the problem is too big. He might tell you that you should quit going to church, quit living by the Word, quit the things you have been taught, quit living God's way, quit on your marriage, quit on your kids, quit on overcoming addiction. You don't have to listen to him. Get the right perspective. Get God's perspective through His Word. And then walk into your Promised Land like you own the place.

SIX

DON'T LET IT GET YOU DOWN (PART I)

FIGHT DISCOURAGEMENT FROM CIRCUMSTANCES WITH COURAGE

There is pressure on us, as children of God, to embrace the idea that we are not able. Satan wants to stop us by getting us to think we are not able, because then we won't move forward on the path God has for us.

We are able because the Bible says we are able. Paul wrote in 2 Corinthians 12:10, "For the sake of Christ, then, I am content with weaknesses, insults, hardships, persecutions, and calamities. For when I am weak, then I am strong." That word *strong* means, *I am strong, and I am able, and I can.* It's so important that we focus on who we are in Christ, rather than who we are on our own, what family we were born into, where we were raised, what job we work at, or what someone else says about us.

Do you see yourself as a child of God? I see myself as a child of God first, more than any other definition or label I could give myself. There was a time in my life when seeing myself that way was maybe third or fourth on the list; but over the years, I've learned to care more about God's opinion and God's valuation of me. That means my choices, my decisions, my attitudes, the way I walk, the way I prioritize, the way I live, the way I think, and the way I act are all influenced by the reality that, first and foremost, I am a child of God. I am in this world, but I am not of this world (John 17:14, 16). The world does not generate my emotions or my likes or dislikes.

That's important because we don't always feel like we are able, especially when we're facing impossible situations or when we've just tried something and failed. And yet, God's Word declares we are able. Even in our weakness, we are able and capable in Christ and His strength. If we know we are able, we will also be brave. The two are connected. Fear tells us we aren't able; if we believe fear, we will turn down the path of cowardice. But if we listen to God's opinion of us, if we understand that in Him we are able, then fear will find no place in us.

The Bible is full of exhortations to be brave, to take courage, and to take heart. Courage is an essential ingredient for finishing strong. Courage is what keeps us from waving the white flag.

What do we call losing courage? *Discouragement.* Literally, to be discouraged is *to have our courage stripped away*. To lose it. To have our hearts taken out. To step back from courage and into fear. Or to use our definition above, it's to turn out to be a coward. Discouragement is the process of losing our bravery because we think we aren't able.

Discouragement through circumstances causes us to doubt our abilities when we face darkness, wilderness, challenges, and storms. We must cling to the truths that God is with us, He will fight for us, and He won't let us sink. God gives us the ability and courage to overcome any discouragement that comes our way.

COURAGE IN DARKNESS

When going through tough times and periods of darkness, it's tempting to think God is absent. *Where is God when I need Him the most?* He's right there with you. He always has been; He always will be. God doesn't leave. When trouble comes to the front door, the Lord doesn't go out the back door.

Psalm 23, one of the most famous Scriptures in the Bible, says: "Even though I walk through the valley of the shadow of death, I will fear no evil, for you are with me" (Psalm 23:4). When the psalmist went through the valley, God didn't say, "Oh, wait a minute. I can do a lot of things, but I'm not going through there. That's the valley of the shadow of death. Now, if you find another path, I'll meet you over there; but I'm not going through that valley."

One of the greatest cures I've found for discouragement is seen in the life of David, the author of Psalm 23. You might be familiar with the story of David; he was a shepherd who eventually became the greatest king in Israel's history.

At one point, David and all his men, along with their families and possessions, were in the city of Ziklag in the region of the Philistines. While David and his men were away at battle, another nation, the Amalekites, raided the city. They burned the city, kidnapped their families, and stole their possessions.

When David and his men returned, they found the devastation. They all wept until they had no more power to weep (see 1 Samuel 30:4). The Bible says, "David was greatly distressed, for the people spoke of stoning him, because all the people were bitter in soul, each for his sons and daughters" (verse 6). Because of the bitterness and sorrow, the people began to talk about stoning David. Watch out for bitterness. It springs up in a discouraged heart. Would killing David get their wives and children back? No. But bitterness makes for poor logic.

Look how David responded, though. "But David strengthened himself in the Lord his God" (verse 6). Some versions say, "David encouraged himself in the Lord" (KJV). The word *strengthened* or *encouraged* here means he *fastened himself* to the Lord. Discouragement comes to pull you away from the Lord, to pull you away from God's Word, to pull you away from your relationship with God, to make you think Jesus is letting you down. Satan will try to separate you from Jesus. David pushed through that and fastened himself to the Lord. That means he took courage. He found strength. He had become discouraged, but he got his courage back.

I think David probably found a spot where he could be alone and spent some time being completely honest with God. I imagine he said something like this: "Lord, I don't know what happened with these men of mine, but I'm not walking away from you. Those men are bitter and discouraged, but I'm not turning away from you. I'm staying right here with you. I don't like what's happening now, but I know somehow, some way, you're going to help me."

One of the truths that has most empowered me to

get back up when life didn't play along is simply this: you can choose to recover. Discouragement is not irreversible. It might feel like it is, but you can find courage again. And the choice is yours. There is a lot of hope in that: it means you are not a victim of your circumstances.

David wept until there was no power to weep. He was sorrowful, and with good reason. That's normal, necessary, and healthy. But he didn't stay there. At some point he said, "That's it. I choose to recover. I still miss my wife and my kids. I don't have any of my possessions. And I'm going to do my best to recover what I lost. But I'm strong in the Lord. I'm okay in Him. I cannot get up from this place of hurt and pain and sadness and potential bitterness unless I decide that right here, right now, I'm going to get better. I choose courage; I choose to recover."

That is so powerful! You can choose to recover before you feel recovered and before you look recovered. I've done it, and so can you! It's a choice, and you have the power to make that choice.

Jesus said, "In the world you have trouble and suffering, but take courage—I have conquered the world" (John 16:33 NET). That means discouragement and courage can coexist. Just because discouragement comes in doesn't mean courage has to leave. It's just that our focus tends to move toward discouragement. Shift it back to courage. Reject discouragement and choose courage.

I don't think David stopped being sad or mad. But instead of letting those emotions paralyze him or lead him into making dumb decisions, which is what his men were about to do, David found courage in God and turned his emotions toward winning the fight. He fastened himself to God, chose to be okay, and stepped back into the battle.

Sometimes we need to pat ourselves on the back. We can be so hard on ourselves. No one is perfect. There will always be reasons to second-guess our decisions, regret our mistakes, or feel like we've let people down. But we can't let those things discourage us. I'm sure David was wondering, *Why didn't I have more people on guard? Why did I leave everyone unprotected?* One of the signs of good leaders is that they are able to process failure, put negativity aside, and look toward the future.

Notice the source of David's encouragement, though. David didn't strengthen himself in his logic or strategies. He didn't strengthen himself in his military might. He didn't strengthen himself in *himself* at all. He found strength in God. First in private, then by going to the priest and seeking guidance for his next steps (1 Samuel 30:7-8).

COURAGE IN THE WILDERNESS

Once Israel decided they were too frightened to enter the Promised Land, God informed them that no one who had exited Egypt would enter the Promised Land, essentially waiting for the doubters to die so the next generation could grow up and fulfill God's call (Numbers 14:23). It sounds harsh, but it was actually mercy. God could have just wiped them out and started over, but instead He miraculously led, fed, and protected them for the next four decades. He was far more committed to the promise than they were, and He wasn't going to give up. He just had to find people who wouldn't give up, either.

While in the desert, there were many more opportunities to become discouraged. God knew that, and He was watching out for them. Numbers 21:4 says, "Then they journeyed from Mount Hor by the Way of the Red Sea, to go around the land of Edom; and the soul of the people became very discouraged on the way" (NKJV).

They had to go "around the land of Edom." God didn't want Israel to have to fight Edom, so He took them the long way. That didn't sit well with Israel. They were tired, and they started getting frustrated with God. The Hebrew word translated *discouraged* here means *filled with anxiety, annoyed, shortness of spirit, depression because of oppression*. They became irritated, impatient, and depressed.

I wonder how often depression is a direct result of discouragement? At times in my life, I have battled depression. Thank God I got the victory, but, at the time, I didn't know what I was feeling. Now, looking back, I know I was discouraged. I was discouraged because the path I was on was taking too long. I expected quicker results, and when the path was longer and more difficult than I thought it would be, I grew discouraged and then depressed.

I remember thinking things like, *I don't understand. I'm a better preacher than that guy. Why is his church growing and I'm stuck? What's the deal?* We believed God was asking us as a church to do things certain ways, but we would see other churches do things differently and grow very quickly. It was confusing. Now, forty-plus years later, we're still here, and many of them are not. Again, that's not judgmental. I'm grateful God took the time to build strong foundations in our church, even though it wasn't always fun or flashy.

Often the paths God sets us on will look like the

long way to us. But it's the right way. We have to trust in the Lord with all our heart and lean not on our own understanding (see Proverbs 3:5). His ways are always the best ways, but sometimes it takes a while for us to see the results. We can't allow ourselves to become annoyed at God's way or impatient with His process.

On a more personal level, for several years I faced a difficult challenge with regard to anger and bitterness. I was the target of serious aggression and false accusations, yet I felt like God was telling me to love my enemies, pray for those who spitefully used me, and bless those who cursed me (see Matthew 5:44). You'd think that would be easy for a pastor, but it wasn't. It was one of the hardest things I had to do, and it didn't help that every time I chose to forgive someone, they would say or do something else to hurt me. It was annoying. I grew impatient. I didn't want to forgive—I wanted to fight. I was frustrated and discouraged with the process because I didn't see the importance of it at the time.

I do now. I still don't like that verse very much (the one about loving your enemies). God knows. But I have a lot of peace with it because now, years later, I see why He had me walk down that path. If I had hated and cursed those who opposed me, I would have stayed connected to them emotionally for the rest of my life. But now I'm not connected to them. I'm free. God severed that chain. I'm not living attached to the past, so I can go full speed into the future. Now I can see why He had me take the long way around, because the short way—continuing to hate, curse, and want revenge—was going to destroy me.

The nation of Israel could not go through the

Edomites because they were not yet strong enough to overcome them. So, they had to go around them. They would come back later and overcome them, but, for now, it wasn't the right time. God knew that, and He chose the right path for them. We need to take courage and trust His timing and His promises.

COURAGE IN THE MIDST OF CHALLENGES

One of the most fascinating passages you'll ever read about courage is found in the book of Joshua. To give you a little context, Israel was camped at the Jordan River, the border of the Promised Land, and they were ready to cross over and conquer the land. Moses, the great leader of Israel, had died, and Joshua was the new leader. Joshua and Caleb had tried to convince Israel to enter forty years earlier, but the nation refused. So, Joshua was more than ready. He'd been waiting most of his life to do this.

But God knew Joshua needed more than just emotions and dreams. He needed courage. He needed an unshakeable commitment to God and to the battle ahead. He needed to burn the white flag. So, God spoke to Joshua, and in eight verses, He said the same thing three times:

"Be strong and courageous" (Joshua 1:6).

"Only be strong and very courageous" (verse 7).

"Have I not commanded you? Be strong and courageous" (verse 9).

God doesn't waste words. When He is redundant, it's on purpose. Joshua was going to face moments when his strength and courage were going be what kept him going. One of the definitions of the word *strong* as it is used in the Bible is to *continue to insist* on things. So, God was saying to Joshua, "As you go, I want you to insist and persevere; I want you to keep on being brave."

Why would God need to tell Joshua that? Because waiting for Israel in the Promised Land were thirty-one strong cities ruled by thirty-one powerful kings, and he was going to have to face them all. The Promised Land was not just there for the taking. It was inhabited, and the people who lived there were powerful. It's as if God was telling Joshua, "You're going to come across kings, cities, and giants. But don't you dare think you are not able. That's what the previous generation thought, and it kept them from entering into the promise. Don't turn coward when you face those temptations, tests, and trials. Joshua, you are able, and you need to know that. I promised to give you the land. Here it is. Now go get it."

That's the Charles Neiman expanded version of the conversation, but I think it gives the sense of the passage. This story illustrates something important for us. Often, if you have been given a promise of God, you still have to conquer some things in order to enjoy the promise in your life. Some things are easier to conquer than others, but just like Joshua, we are going to need to insist on some things. We are going to need courage that is strong and bravery that doesn't run out. And just as He was with Joshua, so God is with us throughout the process.

COURAGE IN THE STORM

You've probably read or heard the story of Peter walking on the water, found in Matthew 14. Peter and the disciples were on a boat in the middle of a large lake when a storm came up. It wasn't just any storm, either. These were experienced fishermen, and the wind and waves were so terrifying they were convinced they were going to die.

Suddenly, when they had essentially given up, they saw Jesus walking on the water. At first they thought He was a ghost. I imagine that only confirmed their fears of imminent death. Jesus called out to them and assured them He wasn't the Grim Reaper—He was just their best friend . . . out for a walk . . . on the water . . . in the middle of a storm. And why not? He's God.

Peter called out to Jesus and asked Him, if He was really Jesus, to command Peter to come to Him on the water. Personally, I've never understood Peter's logic with that request, but I probably wouldn't be thinking clearly in his situation either. Jesus told Peter to come to Him, so Peter did. And for a few moments, he stayed on the surface. He gets a lot of flak for what happened next, but I think we should remember that, at least temporarily, Peter walked on water. He had courage; you have to give him credit for that.

Matthew (who incidentally was watching from the safety of the boat), records what happened next. "So, Peter got out of the boat and walked on the water and came to Jesus. But when he saw the wind, he was afraid, and beginning to sink he cried out, 'Lord, save me'" (Matthew 14:29-30).

Jesus reached out to Peter, took hold of him, and

then said, "O you of little faith, why did you doubt?" (verse 31). They got into the boat, the wind ceased, and all the disciples worshiped Jesus.

Notice at what moment Peter sank. Not when he stepped out of the boat, but rather when he took his eyes off Jesus and started looking at the storm. I'm not saying don't ever look at your circumstances; I'm saying don't fix your eyes on your circumstances. Being aware of what's happening around you is wisdom, but be careful to not fixate on your circumstances so long you forget who told you to step out in the first place. Take stock of your situation, make plans, get advice, and brainstorm strategies—but don't let anything less than Jesus hold your gaze.

The problem wasn't that Peter didn't have courage. It was that he lost it when he needed it most. And he lost it because the storm captivated him more than Jesus did. This happens to us too. Sometimes we are more awestruck by the power of the wind and the waves than we are by the power of the Creator of the universe.

We lose our courage the same way Peter did: by letting wind and waves capture our focus. Jesus told a parable about wind and waves in Matthew 7:

> Everyone then who hears these words of mine and does them will be like a wise man who built his house on the rock. And the rain fell, and the floods came, and the winds blew and beat on that house, but it did not fall, because it had been founded on the rock. And everyone who hears these words of mine and does not do

> them will be like a foolish man who built his house on the sand. And the rain fell, and the floods came, and the winds blew and beat against that house, and it fell, and great was the fall of it. (verses 24-27)

In other words, outside pressures, problems, and threats will come against us. If our lives are founded on Jesus and His Word, we won't give in. But if we try to withstand those things on the basis of our own opinions or resources, we won't last.

Wind is invisible, yet it's loud, threatening, and often powerful. What winds do we face in our lives? Winds such as fear, doubt, skepticism, uncertainty, rumors, philosophies, and false doctrine. Paul writes that we should grow into maturity and "no longer be children, tossed to and fro by the waves and carried about by every wind of doctrine" (Ephesians 4:14). We have to be careful not to be carried away by winds that are contrary to God's Word.

It's amazing how quickly a storm can turn a tranquil ocean into a raging, roiling mess. Similarly, our circumstances can change almost instantly. We can feel threatened and overwhelmed, like we're sinking in life's waters. But we must remember that the winds and waves of life have no power over Jesus. He walks on the waves. He stills the wind. If we are going to keep our courage, we have to learn to keep our eyes on Jesus. We have to believe Him when He says, "Come! You can do this!" We have to believe His Word.

Jesus is in the business of healing discouraged hearts. We will inevitably walk through darkness, wilderness, challenges, and storms, and these circumstances will discourage us and tempt us to wave the white flag. During these times, we must remember that God is with us, He will fight for us, He has a plan for us, and He won't let us sink. He brings us healing and courage; it's part of His mission and job description. He said in Luke 4:18, "He has sent Me to heal the brokenhearted" (NKJV). If you are battling discouragement, He is your source of strength. Just like David, the Israelites, Joshua, and Peter, you can find your faith again. You can find hope, courage, and direction to face whatever trials and tests have come your way.

SEVEN

DON'T LET IT GET YOU DOWN (PART 2)

FIGHT DISCOURAGEMENT FROM PEOPLE WITH CONFIDENCE

When I was in college, I worked at a pool as a lifeguard over the summer. I taught little kids how to swim. It was hilarious and so much fun, and I was good at it. When teaching them to swim, half the battle was building up their confidence. The problem wasn't the kids—it was the parents.

I remember one mother in particular. I had her son swimming across the pool. I had him in the deep end, and I had him happily swimming back and forth across the pool. Then she saw him and said, "Oh my god! You can't swim in the deep end." And down he went. I had to jump in and pull the kid out. He was swimming, but he went from able to unable because he took the second opinion.

We just looked at ways that circumstances can discourage us and cause us to want to surrender. Just as God is with us though darkness, challenges, wilderness, and storms, He is also with us when the people around us actively discourage us. This form of discouragement is often the hardest to handle because we have to trust where God is leading, even when people aren't behind us. Discouragement from the people around us can cause us to shrink back and stay where we are, even when God is calling us forward.

God calls us to be confident when discouragement comes our way. He wants us to be so caught up in Him and in His plans for our lives that when anyone challenges or discourages us, we are able to keep on our path and stay in the race.

TALL POPPY SYNDROME

As we have seen, one of the greatest enemies of endurance is discouragement. Israel struggled with that to the point that an entire generation was not able to take possession of God's promises for them.

The English word *discouraged* has several definitions or nuances. First, it means *to be deprived of courage and hope.* Hope is one of God's great gifts to us. He has a hope and a future for us (Jeremiah 29:11), and hope is the anchor of our souls (Hebrews 6:19). The Bible says, "faith is confidence in what we hope for and assurance about what we do not see" (Hebrews 11:1 NIV). But if we don't have hope, there is nothing for our faith to attach itself to.

Discouragement also means *to lose your confidence.* Our confidence is the basis of our confession of faith. We believe, therefore we speak (see 2 Corinthians 4:13). If we lose our confidence, we lose our voice. We lose our ability and motivation to speak life into the situations and people around us.

Discouragement means to *dishearten or to take your heart out*. What disheartens us? Usually some unhelpful person telling us that our plans and purposes will probably fail. Sometimes, the voice is inside our own head. But more often than not it's another person—friend, enemy, family member, church member, boss, stranger—who felt it was time to take us down a notch because we were too excited about life.

Discouragement tends to be contagious. Discouraged people discourage people, so we have to guard our hearts. We have to be careful how we speak to others and also who we let speak into our lives. Ten discouraged spies managed to poison the attitudes of two million people. That's a frightening fact.

It's hard for me to understand people who don't want to strive for the best in their lives, but it's far harder for me understand people who don't want *others* to win, either. It seems that anyone who dares to dare greatly, anyone who is willing to take a risk or dream bigger than "normal"—whatever that is—should be prepared for a lot of unsolicited and unwanted advice. And by advice, I mean criticism, negativity, doomsaying, and other generally discouraging comments designed to bring you back down to your previous definition of "normal" for your life, or their opinion of what your "normal" should be.

The people who give this "advice" are often good-hearted. I'm giving them the benefit of the doubt here; they think they are helping. They are trying to keep us from getting hurt, or from making fools of ourselves, or from failing. But what they don't understand is we have an inner desire to win. We have a calling and a grace on our lives to do more and accomplish more.

Australian friends of mine have told me that in Australia, people use the phrase *tall poppy.* It was originally a literary reference to someone who is influential or powerful and therefore a threat to the status quo, but, over time, it has come to refer to anyone successful who has an attitude of superiority about their success. My friends tell me that often anyone who is highly confident in their calling and potential, or anyone perceived to have dreams that are too big or daring, or anyone who has too much success or media attention becomes a target of tall poppy syndrome. *Tall poppy syndrome* is the tendency of everyone else to try to cut that person down to size. The thought is that in a field of poppies, you cut the tallest ones, the best ones, the ones that stand out. So, if you see someone who puts on airs, you should remind them they are no better than anyone else by cutting others down. Unfortunately, this happens everywhere, not just in poppy fields and the Land Down Under. Some people seem to like nothing more than attacking anyone who dares to take a risk or to dream bravely. So, if you want to play it safe, don't stand out. Don't grow too much or attempt too much. Don't dream too big or aim too high. Because if you do, someone will try to take you out.

I've been pastoring for well over forty years now, and every time our church has stepped out and attempted something great, well-intentioned naysayers have felt obligated to try to discourage us. When we first decided to rent a little space for our fledgling church, people said,

"Things are going great in this borrowed space. Why would you sign a lease? Why would you pay for furniture? You're going to get in over your head."

Nearly four decades ago, a pastor here in El Paso came to see me. He was a nice man, an older gentleman who had been here for many years. We were growing as a church, God was doing exciting things, and we were building a new church building. It was a huge step.

I said, "Sir, I'm so honored. May I ask why you came to see me?"

He replied, "I've heard about what God is doing at your church. It's really beautiful."

"Thank you."

He continued, "It's a great thing to see. But you know, back in the day, when I started, I had big dreams like you do now. I had a big vision like you have. So, when I heard what you are doing, I really felt that I needed to come and tell you that it's not going to work. You really should rethink buying all that land and building that building. The people of El Paso are not going to go for this. The people of El Paso don't believe in big, nice things. You already have a good building downtown. It's easy. You can take care of it. You ought to stay right where you are and be happy right where you are, because you're probably going to fail, and then you're going to have a lot of debt. I believe I'm supposed to help you not get hurt like I was hurt."

You can imagine how encouraged I felt when he left. I believe he came with a good heart, but he came with a discouraged heart. His discouragement was trying to jump on me because misery loves company.

When we built what is now our main campus, the

facilities were beautiful and very large, especially in comparison to what people had seen or expected from a church in El Paso, Texas. I know the miracles and the generosity of people that brought that building into existence, but some people literally couldn't believe a church could accomplish that, and rumors started flying around that we were doing something illegal. There was no reason or basis for the rumors.

Years later, looking back on comments and drama like that, it's easy to laugh it off. To say, "You're entitled to your opinion, but whatever. I'm just glad I didn't stop." But in the moment, when friends you care about and people in positions of influence are making sideways comments or outright accusations, it can be hard to take. You start to think, *I have to fight my own fears, the devil, the circumstances . . . and now people I trusted?*

I've heard similar comments from people in my church for over forty years now. "Pastor, I don't understand what happened. I started following God and going to church, and the Lord is doing something good in my life. But now my family is mad. My friends are mad. The people at work call me Bible Boy and Hallelujah Boy and Bible Thumper. They ask me what's wrong with me, they tell me I'm crazy, and they tell me I don't know how to enjoy life. And their definition of living life is on Friday, when they get paid, they fill up the back of the pickup with beer and stand on the street corner and drink when they should be home with their wife and their kids. They drink up the rent and they drink up the diaper money. Then they tell me they know how to live, and that I'm the crazy one. *I'm the crazy one?*"

I have learned that the people who have achieved the least in life tend to be the most critical of those who are trying to do something more than they did. If valuing their opinion means I've got to sit with them on the sidelines, then I'm not going to value their opinion. In fact, I'm going to hold their opinion in contempt, and I'm going to go for the abundant life Jesus has placed in front of me. That's not condescending. That's choosing whose voice to listen to and whose opinion to value. Researcher and author Brené Brown said this in her book *Daring Greatly*:

> A lot of cheap seats in the arena are filled with people who never venture onto the floor. They just hurl mean-spirited criticisms and put-downs from a safe distance. The problem is, when we stop caring what people think and stop feeling hurt by cruelty, we lose our ability to connect. But when we're defined by what people think, we lose the courage to be vulnerable. Therefore, we need to be selective about the feedback we let into our lives. For me, if you're not in the arena also getting your butt kicked, I'm not interested in your feedback.[7]

People will try to shame us. They'll try to accuse us. They'll call us names. That's not fun at all—it hurts to be ridiculed or rejected. It hurts to be disrespected. And that's the point. That's why they do it. They want to change our minds and our actions. They want us to conform to their way of living. Maybe they're malicious, and maybe they're not—but our boldness, courage, and success remind them they are still where they've always been, stuck in mediocrity. If they can hold us back, maybe they won't feel so bad about themselves.

We can't hold back just because others won't move forward. Somehow, we have to be fighters without being mean, ugly, or resentful. You have to strive for a win, but you also have to rest in Jesus. It's one of those dichotomies in Scripture that can only be resolved when you realize who you are in Jesus and what He does for you. The truth is, people around us need us to be all we can be in Jesus, whether they understand it or not. If you're called to stand out and to lead, then do it. Be a tall poppy, but without the arrogance. Be confident but not proud. Be strong but not abrasive. Be brave but not foolhardy. Lead with empathy and vulnerability. Don't let others cut you down to their level; seek to help others grow as tall as you.

SIDELINED

In a previous chapter we talked about how the Israelites, on the brink of the Promised Land, were discouraged by their leaders and unable to enter the Promised Land due to their doubt. They listened to the wrong sources of information, and that discouraged them and knocked their confidence to the point that they were sidelined. They missed out on what God had for them. How did that happen? How did a nation that had seen firsthand some of the most spectacular miracles in the Bible end up doubting and ultimately rejecting the God who performed them?

We do the exact same thing though. When we deal with discouragement from time to time, it is amazing how quickly our confidence can vanish. One moment we feel on top of the world, and the next moment we think the world is falling apart.

The ten spies discouraged all two million people—minus two. They couldn't sway Joshua and Caleb. Midway through the ten spies' negative report, the Bible says Caleb jumped in and contradicted them: "But Caleb quieted the people before Moses and said, 'Let us go up at once and occupy it, for we are well able to overcome it'" (Numbers 13:30). Joshua and Caleb stood up to the lies of defeat, and they did their best to convince others not to give up on God's promise and plan for them.

Although Caleb and Joshua were not listened to immediately, they remain faithful and become confident leaders who eventually lead the Israelites into the Promised Land. I pray we would become a people who reject discouragement and stand for faith.

EIGHT

SEEING CLEARLY

FIGHT DISTRACTIONS WITH VISION

We've looked at how the negative perception of Israel kept them out of the Promised Land. Now I'd like to look at how Israel entered the Promised Land under the leadership of Joshua. The story starts in Joshua 1.

> After the death of Moses the servant of the Lord, the Lord said to Joshua the son of Nun, Moses' assistant, "Moses my servant is dead. Now therefore arise, go over this Jordan, you and all this people, into the land that I am giving to them, to the people of Israel. Every place that the sole of your foot will tread upon I have given to you, just as I promised to Moses." (verses 1-3)

Notice the verb tense of the last sentence. "Every place that the sole of your foot will tread upon I *have given* to you." That's a past-tense verb. In other words, God is looking at the conquest as if it were a finished act in His mind. That's important.

God continues speaking with Joshua:

> "From the wilderness and this Lebanon as far as the great river, the river Euphrates, all the land of the Hittites to the Great Sea toward the going down of the sun shall be your territory. No man shall be able to stand before you all the days of your life. Just as I was with Moses, so I will be with you. I will not leave you or forsake you. Be strong and courageous, for you shall cause this people to inherit the land that I swore to their fathers to give them." (verses 4-6)

Finally, they are going into the Promised Land, and Joshua will lead them into their inheritance. The first generation was unable to enter, not because God didn't want them to, but because they had a wrong perception of themselves. They saw themselves as grasshoppers, to be exact. And Moses could not assuage their doubts.

My question is this: how was Joshua able to lead the second generation differently? After all, Moses was an incredible leader. It wasn't his fault the first generation blew their chance. What did this second generation have that enabled them to believe and obey? How was Joshua able to motivate and inspire them? The difference was that this group had clear vision. God gave Joshua and Israel a clear description of the land they were to inherit and the level of victory they would achieve. He told them the boundaries. He told them no one would be able to stand before them.

Proverbs 29:18 says: "Where there is no vision, the people perish" (KJV). That word *vision* refers to a divine or prophetic revelation. Many people don't have vision for their lives. They don't have a plan, and they're not really moving toward anything definite and purposeful. They look ahead to the weekend and that's about it. They don't have vision for their marriage, their kids, their friendships, their finances, or their spiritual walk. "The people perish" can be translated as *cast off restraint, run wild,* or *destroyed.* Not having vision plays into the devil's hands, because he comes to steal, kill, and destroy (see John 10:10).

Just as God gave Israel vision, He wants to give us vision. We need a vision painted by the Holy Spirit on the canvas of our hearts. Ask yourself: *Do I have vision? Is there purpose to my life? Do I have clear goals, and am I moving toward those goals? Is my life accomplishing something? Am I intentional and effective in what I do?* God has a vision for your life, and we've seen it already. It's found in the second half of John 10:10. "I came that they may have life and have it abundantly." God's vision is life—abundant life. His vision needs to be our vision. We should be moving toward the life Jesus came to give us.

Courage is not enough. It must be attached to vision. Just because we are brave, bold, and pumped up doesn't mean we will end up in the right place. We have to know where we are going. Conversely, vision is not enough, either. Vision without courage is one of the most frustrating, condemning things you can have, because you know what you're supposed to be doing, but you aren't brave enough to do it.

That's why God told Joshua the plan, and then He reiterated the need for boldness. We read this earlier. God says in Joshua 1:6, "Be strong and courageous." Then in verse 7, "Only be strong and very courageous." And yet again in verse 9: "Have I not commanded you? Be strong and courageous." Then the people add in their encouragement:

> "All that you have commanded us we will do, and wherever you send us we will go. Just as we obeyed Moses in all things, so we will obey you. Only may the Lord your God be with you, as he was with Moses! Whoever rebels against your commandment and disobeys your words, whatever you command him, shall be put to death. Only be strong and courageous." (verses 16-18)

Can you see the power of a God-given vision combined with courage? It's unstoppable.

GET ON THE FIELD

Vision is exciting and inspiring, but without corresponding *action*, it's just a cute dream. If you truly have vision and courage, it should produce movement. Israel didn't just sit around the locker room high-fiving one other and talking a big game. They got out on the field and worked as hard as they could. They took risks. They made sacrifices. They believed the vision, and it produced visible, measurable results.

I was at a friend's house a long time ago, and I was in the kitchen with my friend and his wife. I couldn't help but notice there was a picture of a swimsuit model on the refrigerator. And it wasn't a picture of the wife, either. My friend saw me notice the picture and he said,

"That's not there for me." We all laughed.

His wife spoke up. "It's there for me. I'm going to look like that model someday. I'm going to get in shape. That's why I put it on the refrigerator, so every time I'm tempted to open the door and eat something I shouldn't, I'll stay motivated."

"Good for you," I said.

The husband said good-naturedly, "Tell Charles how long that picture has been on the refrigerator."

The wife looked a bit sheepish. "Five years."

We all got another good laugh out of that. It's clear, though, that a picture on a refrigerator doesn't have the power to change you. At some point you have to change. You have to pay the price, get rid of distractions, and do the hard work.

When I was eight years old, I somehow talked my dad into buying me a little weight set. I've been lifting weights ever since. I work out five times a week, and exercise has always been important to me. Sometimes people tell me, "Pastor, you've inspired me. I want to get in shape. I've even joined a gym!"

Then I'll see them a couple months later, and nothing has changed. And I'll say, "How's the workout routine going?"

"Well, I joined the gym, but I don't really go . . ."

Life is busy, and there are a lot of things shouting for our time, energy, and money. But we all know you don't get fit because you joined a gym. There's only one way to get in shape: you have to do the work. And you have to do it for a significant amount of time. Only then will you see the results.

Keep in mind, the story of Joshua covers many years, probably twenty-five to thirty by many estimates. Taking possession of God's promises was a process that required ongoing action. It was action motivated by vision and characterized by courage, but it was also hard work. Remember what Hebrews 12 says: we run the race with perseverance. It's a marathon, and we have to pace ourselves. We have to be in this for the long haul.

Proverbs says, "All hard work brings a profit, but mere talk leads only to poverty" (Proverbs 14:23 NIV). Again, if you truly have vision and courage, you'll have action. You'll put in the work. On the flipside, if you find yourself not taking action to reach your goals, take a look at your vision and at your courage level.

CAREFUL TO DO

If vision and action are so important, how do we get them? God addressed this when He spoke to Joshua. First, He told Joshua to be brave, and then He told him exactly how to live and think in order to receive the promises of God.

> "Be strong and very courageous. Be careful to obey all the law my servant Moses gave you; do not turn from it to the right or to the left, that you may be successful wherever you go. Keep this Book of the Law always on your lips; meditate on it day and night, so that you may be careful to do everything written in it. Then you will be prosperous and successful." (Joshua 1:7-8 NIV)

God told Joshua (and He tells us) not to turn to the right or the left from His ways. Success and prosperity come from obeying God. It's really as simple as that. When we are in harmony with His design, we will walk in the abundant life Jesus came to give us.

That doesn't mean everything will be easy, which is why the Bible is full of exhortations to not surrender or faint. On this side of heaven, some things just won't work right, because sin and its consequences have invaded earth. Sorrow and pain are part of our existence. Death happens. But that doesn't mean we can't experience a great level of God's abundant life here on earth, with far greater things to come in heaven. God's Word reveals the abundant life He designed for us. It is intensely practical, and it addresses every pain point we might be facing.

Verse 8 says we are to "be careful to do everything written" in the Scriptures, and that if we do, we will be prosperous and successful. We have to make sure our vision is informed by God's Word. We have to make an effort to find out what His laws are and think about how to apply them to our lives. Meditating in the Word keeps us on track. We're not distracted. We stay in our lanes on the freeway. We don't pull off the road for "sideshow distractions" (Proverbs 4:25 MSG) that try to take our focus off God's Word.

Obedience is not an accident. It starts with finding out how God wants you to live, in His Word. Ephesians 5:10 says, "Find out what pleases the Lord" (NIV). Once we discover the right way to live in a specific area, we step out in faith and obey. As husbands and wives, if we are careful to live the way God tells us, our marriages will succeed. As businesspeople, if we act and talk and treat people the way God tells us to, our businesses will experience greater prosperity. As parents, if we raise our kids according to God's Word, we will raise happy, healthy, mature kids. God's ways work. We just have to be careful to do them.

THE INNER BATTLE

Read what God told Joshua again: "Keep this Book of the Law always on your lips; meditate on it day and night, so that you may be careful to do everything written in it. Then you will be prosperous and successful" (Joshua 1:8 NIV). One of the key words in God's instructions to Joshua is the word *meditate*. We read that word and don't think much about it, but put yourself in Joshua's sandals for a moment. He was about to lead an army into war. I'm sure his adrenaline was pumping. He probably had his assistant outside the tent, sharpening his sword. He was more than ready for action. Yet God told him to crack open the Bible and study it. That's probably the last thing Joshua was thinking: *We're on the brink of war. I think I'll go study my Bible.*

God wasn't just talking about a one-time Bible study, of course. He was teaching Joshua that he needed a lifestyle of knowing and obeying the Word. God knew Joshua had decades of battle ahead of him. But instead of giving him battle strategies or telling him to go check on his army, He told him to pay attention to his inner battles.

We all have inner activity and outer activity, inner enemies and outer enemies, inner battles and outer battles. We often pay more attention to the outer ones and neglect the inner ones. That's exactly why God said, "Joshua, don't neglect the inner battle. Don't forget the inner man. Meditate on the Word, and it will make your actions, your decisions, your leadership, and your battles successful."

I've had people say, "Pastor, I don't get paid to study my Bible like you do. I don't have time to sit around and read the Word. I have to bring home a paycheck." I've got news for you. Joshua didn't have time, either. You think you have pressure at work? Joshua's job involved fighting thirty-one kings and leading a couple million cranky Israelites into a foreign country. Plus he had a wife and children of his own. He was a busy guy. He didn't live in a fairy tale world. He didn't sit in his tent and meditate all day. He was out on the battlefield. He was leading the army, making decisions, and administrating an entire nation. He was busy, but he did what he needed to do internally so he could have success externally. Don't let busyness distract you from putting in the hard work to keep your vision.

It's the internal battle that usually causes us to quit. The external battles are tough, but if our souls are healthy and encouraged, we can face astounding odds without giving in. But if our internal selves are unhealthy, if we start losing the battle on the inside, even small challenges can overwhelm us, make our vision blurry, and make us wave the white flag.

Vision and courage produce action, but don't let action distract you from the inner battle. As you're fighting battles, overcoming enemies, and pursuing the abundant life of Jesus, stay connected to the Word.

I think "day and night" simply means *at every opportunity and in every way*. Make every effort to spend time in Scripture, but find what works for you. Maybe it's in the morning before everyone wakes up. Maybe it's in the car on the way to work. Maybe it's by listening to the Bible on audio. Maybe it's by studying and praying with a close friend. Maybe it's by taking a class or reading a book that helps you understand the Word better.

What are you meditating on? Is it the culture around you? A television show? A popular philosophy? A problem at work? The stock market? A doctor's report? Sometimes we spend two hours researching some random symptom or rumor online, but we can't find fifteen minutes to read a couple chapters of the Bible. I'm not being critical—just real. It happens to us all. Are you taking time to discover and meditate on what God says about your situation?

In order to keep your vision clear and centered around God's Word, there are three things you must do:

1. Take your thoughts captive.

Our vision is informed by what we think about. God instructs us to put the Word of God on repeat inside our brains. That's what meditation is in the biblical sense. It means to focus our minds on something, to play it over and over, to chew on it. This doesn't happen by accident—we have to be intentional about it.

We meditate on things all day. Things are always revolving in our minds. We replay movie scenes. We replay memories. We replay how great we were twenty-five years ago. We replay special moments, and we replay negative ones too. All of that has its place, but God is saying to take time to do this with His Word as well, regularly and as often as we have opportunity.

What happens when we revolve His Word in our minds? We begin to get understanding and insight into God's will applied to our specific situations. We gain understanding of what is wise and pleasing to God. That understanding equips us to act boldly, to take actions that lead to victory.

Ask yourself, *What do I think about during the day? Am I inserting God into the revolutions of my mind so that I can remain focused and envisioned? Am I familiarizing myself with His Word? Am I taking it into account when I make my decisions?*

At first, you will find you have to train yourself to do it. Why? Because there are thoughts, words, opinions, and belief systems that are already revolving in your mind. These might be thoughts from your childhood. They might be thoughts formed by the opinions of others. They might be thoughts based on tragedies or traumatic events in your life. These thoughts don't want to be replaced—they have been with you for a long time. It may take you a while to force the fear, worry, doubt, unbelief, anxiety, pride, or intimidation out of your thoughts. Don't give up! If you change your thoughts, you'll sharpen your vision.

2. Speak truth to yourself.

God said, "Don't let the word depart from your mouth" (Joshua 1:8). Part of being envisioned is speaking the Word. The Word needs to be in your mouth, not just in your mind.

I do this all the time. Depending on where I am, I'll speak to myself under my breath or even out loud. I do it in my car. I do it when standing in lines. Instead of reading the silly headlines on the magazines in the grocery store as I stand in line, I'll meditate on the Word. I think it in my mind and speak it to myself in a low tone of voice, almost under my breath.

You might be thinking, *People will think I'm crazy*. They don't think you are crazy when you're standing in line singing a song to yourself, or when you're on the phone with someone. I'm not saying to scare people, so use common sense. But you'd be surprised how powerful it can be for your own heart and emotions to hear you speak the Word. When you speak, you hear yourself too. So you get a triple dose of the Word. First you think it, then you speak it, then you hear it. It's a highly effective way to focus your life and vision on the Word of God.

I do this on airplanes all the time. On fourteen-hour flights, I'll spend the first hour or so just going over Scriptures, meditating on them in my mind, speaking them to myself, and listening to them. I'll think about how that Word applies to current situations in my life or to attitudes and feelings I'm having. I'll think about how it applies to my vision and where I want my life to be in five years or ten years. I think about how it applies to the kind of husband, father, grandfather, pastor, and follow of Jesus I want to be.

As I do that, passages of the Bible begin to open up to me like never before. The best way I can explain it is that it's like a shell cracks open. The meaning is made clear, and I see the Bible and my life situation in new ways.

3. Growl like a lion.

We talked earlier about how the devil is like a lion, "seeking someone to devour" (1 Peter 5:8). When you are spending time meditating on God's Word, that is when the devil growls the loudest. But you have a strength he doesn't have. The Hebrew word for *meditate* in Joshua 1:8 can also be translated as *growl*. Don't let the devil intimidate you—growl back. I am not recommending you growl in line at a grocery store, because that definitely will scare people. But there are times in life when you need to get your growl back. If the devil is threatening your vision and telling you that you can't prosper or you are going to fail, growl back at him! Don't back down—stare him down. Stand firm.

The Word of God will produce a response in you, and that response often includes emotion. You'll find courage rising in your heart. You'll feel righteous anger about areas where the devil, sin, or circumstances have tried to limit you or lie to you. Let the Bible fill your vision with strength and truth as you meditate God's promises.

God told Joshua what the result of a Word-focused lifestyle would be: "Then you will be prosperous and successful" (Joshua 1:8 NIV). To *prosper* means *to break forth, to become mighty, to succeed, to be victorious.* That is the opposite of waving the white flag, and it sounds like the kind of lives we all want to have.

You might consider making a list of the things that discourage you and researching what the Bible says about them. Then take time to read and reread those Scriptures. Think about them, understand them, and apply them. Renew your mind. No obstacle or enemy can withstand God's Word. Like Israel, you'll have clear vision and you will be prosperous and successful.

NINE

THE HARDER THEY FALL

FIGHT OPPOSITION WITH GROWTH

God gave Israel the land, just as He had promised. They were able to enter, conquer, and possess the promise. The story is recorded for *us*, though, not them. God wanted us to know that He also has promises for us. He has given us a future and a hope (Jeremiah 29:11). This promised land is the kingdom of God and the abundant life Jesus came to give us. It is the destiny, the calling, the fruit, the purpose God has for our lives. It is the people He has put in our world and the beautiful relationships we are able to build.

Don't believe the lie of the devil that God doesn't have purpose for your life. Don't believe the lie that you blew your chance, that you're too old, or that life has passed you by. It makes me so sad when I see people in their seventies or eighties who feel like their life is now a throw-away life. Your life is never a throw-away life. God always has a purpose for you and you're still growing.

This promised land doesn't come without a fight, though. Just like Israel had to conquer, so we have to conquer. Joshua was fully aware of that, because he had been into the Promised Land forty years earlier. He knew the cities were big, the walls were big, and the people were big. He knew they were facing thirty-one kings and thirty-one armies. He knew the land was probably more fortified than ever because they had spent the last forty years preparing for Israel's invasion.

But that didn't stop him, and it should stop us. Don't let the size of the enemy or the difficulty of the fight discourage you. The bigger the giants, the harder they fall. Joshua was able to not only believe that himself but also to inspire the people to believe it. And it worked. They were successful.

To be honest, I was a bit shocked years ago, when I first came into the kingdom of God, to discover there was opposition to growth. Not just opposition extending God's kingdom, either—opposition to growing in the Lord personally. Most of the opposition has been internal: inner demons, you could say. They've been personal battles I have had to face and overcome in my walk with God as I moved from babyhood to childhood to spiritual adulthood.

I think I had the idea that life as a Christian would be a tip-toeing-through-the-tulips kind of experience. That everything would be great and wonderful because now I was a Christian. I think life *should* be spectacular as a Christian—but that doesn't mean there won't be struggles. We will have to fight the good fight of faith (1 Timothy 6:12).

We each face our own battles, our own kings, our

own giants. But at the end of the day, there are a lot of similarities. Maybe you face yours in your business, or in your health, or in some other area. I'd like to share a few of the kings I've had to conquer over the years, enemies who tried to oppose me and hinder my growth. It's not a long list—thank God I didn't have to conquer thirty-one kings. I hope the things I've learned help you with the challenges you face as well.

REJECTION

Rejection hurts. We all want to be liked, loved, and valued. After all, God is love, and we were created to love and be loved. We weren't meant for rejection. Hatred and betrayal are foreign to God's plan. But sin has twisted the ways humans experience relationship, and we've all suffered hurt, rejection, and hate. Rejection can destroy our confidence and our hope very quickly.

Jesus Himself was rejected and betrayed—and it hurt Him. You can tell by the way He responded to Judas, Peter, the disciples, and the multitudes. He didn't let it stop Him, though, and He didn't let it make Him bitter or cynical. Jesus modeled for us how to face rejection without losing heart.

As a pastor, I've faced my fair share of rejection. I'm sure you've faced your share of rejection too. The reasons and the context might be different, but the pain is the same. The point here is, growth is dependent on how you react. Will you choose to let rejection bring you closer to God, the One who never rejects you, or will you let rejection stunt your progress?

I like to think I'm a nice guy and that our church is wonderful, but not everybody who comes to my church stays at my church. Many do, but over the years, there have been quite a few who have left. There have been some who have visited and didn't come back. And I tend to think, "Wait a minute, to know me is to love me! What's going on here?"

On top of that, I believe God has called me and placed a purpose on my life to help people, to show them His ways, to help them get from A to B to Z in their walk with God, and to take spiritual principles and break them down into simple truths so people can digest them and apply them to their lives before they leave the parking lot. That's my goal in every service. Yet, even with all this effort and studying and praying, some still people say no. And some of them say no rather forcefully, accompanied by strong opinions about what I should change.

For many years, that was tough to overcome. Even now, from time to time, I hear that little voice of insecurity and opposition try to catch my ear. I don't play along with it anymore, though. I don't let it talk to me. I recognize it for what it is.

To some extent, I think feelings of rejection and hurt are inevitable. If you're going to open your heart to people, if you're going to love like Jesus loved, and if you're going to take risks to help people, you'll face some hurt. What's the option? Close your heart off to everyone? That doesn't sound like an abundant life.

There are two simple truths that have helped me continue to love people without taking every rejection to heart. First, not even Jesus made everybody happy. That's not an excuse to make people unhappy on purpose or to run over people's feelings carelessly. But not even Jesus could please everyone or make everyone love Him. If Jesus, the personification of love and perfection, could not keep everybody happy, I suspect you and I aren't going to, either.

Second, to use an old phrase, there are "different strokes for different folks." I had to settle in my heart that I'm not the pastor God has for everyone. Some people need someone else, someone God has not made me to be. He will set them in the right family, with the right pastor, and they will be blessed where He plants them. It won't be with me, but that's okay because it's not about me. It's about people. I have made peace with that truth, but sometimes I have to remind myself of that.

The real heart of rejection is the feeling of insufficiency, of inadequacy. What if I'm not enough? What if you're not enough? We know God has called us, but when people reject us in the area of our calling, it's hard to process. It makes us question our identity, our value, and our future. With every rejection, I used to think, *What if nobody ever likes me again? If nobody ever likes me again, how am I going to fulfill God's calling? If I can't fulfill God's calling, what's going to happen to me at the end of my life?* It got really crazy in my mind and all that craziness kept me from processing what happened in a way that I could grow from.

I learned after a while that there is no reasoning with rejection. You won't always understand it and you can't always fix it. You just learn to deal with it, grow from it, and move on. Again, Jesus Himself faced rejection, so it's only logical we will too. Jesus told His disciples as much.

"Remember the word that I said to you: 'A servant is not greater than his master.' If they persecuted me, they will also persecute you. If they kept my word, they will also keep yours" (John 15:20). In other words, some people will respond to you, and some will reject you. That's reality, so learn to deal with it.

I also learned to be honest with myself. If everyone was rejecting me, or if many people were responding negatively to a certain area of my leadership, I needed to take a look in the mirror. Maybe it wasn't a *them* problem but rather a *me* problem. Maybe there were things about the way I acted, or thought, or responded, or talked that were driving people away.

That's a healthy way to think as a leader, I believe. We're in the people business. We can't just say, "Oh well, it's their loss" every time. We need to learn how to read people's reactions, adjust, grow, and continue onward without going into an emotional tailspin.

LIES

The second king or giant whose opposition I had to overcome in my life was lies. Bald-faced, outright, flat-out lies. I'm not talking about minor misconceptions. I'm talking about people coming up with accusations and lies about me, my family, or our church. They didn't even have any basis in the truth. Then those people would get on the radio or TV or stand in front of their churches and speak those lies as if they came from the Bible.

I look back on some of those lies now, and they're kind of funny. I remember hearing from a man in the church about a conversation he had with his coworker. The coworker said, "I don't know how you can go to that church and listen to Charles Nieman. He's taking all your money, and he bought three Learjets."

The man in our church asked, "How do you know he's got three Learjets?"

This coworker replied, "I drove by his house and saw them."

"You drove by his house and saw them?"

"Yeah."

"Where were they?"

"They were in his backyard."

I laugh at that story now. Sometimes my children and I will recall some of the more ridiculous lies, and they're funny now. But at the time, they were hurtful. And many of them were outright malicious.

I'm sure you've encountered your share of lies. Sometimes people lie to hurt you. They lie to make themselves look better. They lie to break up a relationship between you and somebody else. They lie because they want to get you fired so they can take your job. They lie because they want custody of the kids. They lie because they want more of the inheritance. They lie because they made a mistake somewhere and are looking for someone to take the blame. They lie because they are hurt themselves and so they're lashing out.

Lying is a horrible human trait, and some people are really good at it. They have black belts in lying. They do it so much they don't even know the difference between a lie and the truth anymore. I've seen people who lie when the truth would have served them better. It's just habit.

So, what can we do about lies? The first thing I started doing was telling myself to toughen up. "Toughen up, buttercup" was a phrase I'd use with myself regularly. That doesn't mean I was excusing their behavior. I just wasn't going to go into shock over it.

In my experience, malicious liars usually have some pretty serious internal issues—fear, greed, insecurity, anger—that keep them from truly empathizing with the people they are hurting. I used to wonder: *How could they do this to me? Don't they care about my feelings or reputation?* The answer is that they probably don't care. They're too deceived to see what's happening. Many of them might not even be Christians, so they don't have the same level of sensitivity to the Holy Spirit. Rather than thinking it so strange that they would manifest the works of darkness, I should simply pray for them and let God deal with their lies.

The second thing I did was go to the Bible. I looked at the lies told about Jesus, the lies told about the apostle Paul, the lies told about Peter, James and John, the lies told about God. I'm not the first person who has tried to do good things and been accused of doing bad things. No, I'm just the next in a long and honored tradition.

It's very helpful to notice how Jesus and other heroes of the Bible reacted to lies. Jesus told us to pray for our enemies and love those who treat us spitefully (Matthew 5:44). He modeled it, too—even forgiving those who were crucifying Him while He was hanging on the cross, listening to their jeers. "Father, forgive them, for they do not know what they are doing" (Luke 23:34 NIV).

The third thing I learned is found in Matthew 7:16. Jesus said, "You will know them by their fruits" (NKJV). I remind myself of this a lot. Your fruit speaks for itself. People can call me whatever they want, but they can't deny the results in my life. That's not bragging—it's Bible. We reap what we sow, and if we sow love, integrity, hard work, and a servant heart, that's what our lives will produce in the long run. Even if people temporarily believe a lie, ultimately our fruit cannot be denied, and they will change their minds about us. Let your fruit speak for you. And if you don't see the fruit yet, give it some time. You don't have to correct every error or defend yourself against every accusation. One of Jesus' favorite tactics when He was falsely accused was to not say anything at all. He knew who He was, and He didn't need to prove anything.

Your crazy relatives can say whatever they want, but they can't deny your marriage is getting better. They can't deny your kids are getting better. They can't deny you have more peace. They can't deny that you are not addicted to alcohol anymore. They can't deny the fruit, and if they do, that is a "them" problem. They can't deny your growth; let your fruit prove your character.

The fourth thing I learned is to exercise discernment in the face of lies. Sometimes it's okay to defend yourself when appropriate. That might sound like I'm contradicting myself, because I just said that you should let your fruit speak for you. But there are times when you are given a platform or a place to explain yourself. Peter did that. Paul did that. They gave a defense of their gospel and their actions.

If you don't defend yourself, people are going to believe a lie is the truth. Again, it's not necessary every time, so you have to discern the best strategy. When you know somebody is lying about you, defend yourself. Tell people the truth. Don't sit there and cry. Don't just say, "People ought to know better." They don't know better, and they won't unless you explain what is happening in humility and love. "If they really loved me, they won't believe it." They love you, but they may still believe it. And the reason why they believe it is because you're not saying anything. Defend yourself. You can defend yourself nicely, but defend yourself.

I heard that story about the Learjets, and I decided to address it. The next Sunday, I told the whole church. I could tell that some of them had heard it too, by the nervous laughter in the room. People responded well because they wanted to believe me. They knew me, and the story was ridiculous. They just needed to hear me say it instead of acting like I was scared of it or hiding something.

The final thing I learned about lies is that people only talk about you when you're doing something. That doesn't take away the pain, but it does tell you you're on the right track. Why do dogs bark from behind gates when you walk down the street? Because you're going someplace, and they're stuck in the yard. Critics and liars who attack those who are actually getting things done are nothing but barking dogs. Just walk on past.

POVERTY MENTALITY

The third king I had to conquer was a poverty mentality. Part of that had to do with the way I was raised. I appreciate everything my parents did for us, and I'm thankful, not critical. I was raised in a home where my dad worked very hard and did everything he could. But for much of my childhood, we lived month to month, and some months there was more month than there was paycheck. As a result, close attention was paid to every expense. I understand why, and I'm not judging my parents. But things were watched so closely that there was little, if any, room for fun. They didn't intend it that way, but it created a poverty mindset in me: no matter how much I had, it was never enough. I was always afraid of it running out.

The poverty mentality doesn't just work in people who don't have much. I've known people who were worth millions who were terrified of financial problems. They never had enough to live without fear. If you asked them to help somebody (which I did), they would say, "I'd love to, but I've got to set more aside for my kids." Their kids already had millions in trust funds. It's a never-enough mindset. A poverty mentality does not attach itself to your income, which means it doesn't go away just because you make more money. It attaches itself to your fear. To your feelings of inadequacy. To your need for control. To your lack of trust in God.

It's not here to help, either. You'd think a poverty mentality would be helpful; that it would produce more money and therefore more confidence and peace. But it does the opposite. It squeezes the joy out of life. It robs you of an abundant life. It steals your ability to enjoy what you have, to be content and happy in your current situation. It stunts your spiritual growth.

I realized I had a poverty mentality in my life, and I had to overcome it. I had to quit being afraid of nice things. I had to quit being afraid that if I went on vacation, God would be mad. I had to quit being afraid of giving my tithes and offerings. That was a challenge, and it was a journey. It's more than a one-time decision. You have to train your thoughts and reactions. You create a new mentality: a generosity mentality, a faith mentality.

I'm not talking about not having savings, investments, a college fund, or a retirement plan. I'm talking about never taking your kids to get a scoop of ice cream on Sunday because you're so afraid it's going to break you, and you won't have money to pay the rent. You won't even take your kids to a movie because it's frivolous and unnecessary. You can actually be afraid to love, because love is generous, and a poverty mentality opposes a generous spirit.

Not only did I realize I had to overcome a poverty mindset in myself, I had to overcome one in my city, especially in those early days. I'm not saying I single-handedly overcame poverty, nor am I saying every last person in El Paso had this mindset. But I can't tell you the number of people who said things like this: "Well, you know, Charles, this isn't Dallas. This isn't Houston. This is El Paso, and we're poor." I've learned to distinguish between poverty as an income level and poverty as a mentality. The first one is far easier to escape than the second.

A spirit of generosity invites growth. Philippians 4:19 says, "And my God will supply every need of yours according to his riches in glory in Christ Jesus." Meditate on that. Believe that for yourself, your family, your business, your church, and your city.

INTIMIDATION

The last major king I had to conquer was intimidation. As a child, it seemed like I was always the new kid in school. My dad was in the Army, and by the time I was in tenth grade, I had attended ten different schools. Sometimes I attended three or four different schools in the same year. Everybody else already had friends, and I always felt like the outsider. It created a feeling of intimidation. Intimidation creates a habit of compromise; it pressures you to compromise who you are. It tells you that who you are is not enough: everyone else is somehow better than you, so you need to change.

Like all these kings I had to conquer, overcoming intimidation has been a process. One verse that helped me a lot is Romans 2:11, which says, "God does not show favoritism" (NIV). God loves all of us the same. His promises are for us all. He doesn't rank us or compare us, and He doesn't play favorites. Because we are accepted, valued, and chosen by God, feelings of inferiority or intimidation have no place in us.

Another verse that has encouraged me when I've felt intimidated is Proverbs 18:16: "A man's gift makes room for him and brings him before the great." God has given us the right gifts, and we need to focus on using and improving those gifts rather than trying to be like someone else. True success and influence come when we faithfully do what God created us to do; it is then that we experience true growth.

I'm not suggesting you look at yourself and say, "I'm perfect." No, you're not. You're a work in progress. All of us are continually growing and learning. We need to allow ourselves to be challenged and corrected. We need to be teachable and humble and open. But humility doesn't mean letting others define you. Humility is agreeing with God's definition of you. There will always be people who want to intimidate you. If you know who you are in Christ and build that reality inside of you, you won't be intimidated. You will know your value in God's eyes, and you will stand strong even in the face of opposition. Be who God made you to be, and be proud of who you are in Him. He's proud of you, so agree with Him!

How about you? What kings and giants do you face? What are the biggest forces of opposition in your life? Maybe it's fear, envy, temptation, unforgiveness, bitterness, hate, poor self-image, racism, or bigotry. Be honest with yourself. Then launch an offensive, conquer them, and notice your growth. Your best life is still ahead of you.

TEN

FIGHTING WORDS

FIGHT FALLING BY STANDING FIRM

Joshua had to face thirty-one kings. Thankfully, you and I probably don't have quite that many. In the last chapter I shared some of my personal challenges. Now I'd like to share a few specific Bible passages that have helped me during those challenges and others along the way.

Again, we all face unique challenges. I don't claim to be some superhero model of holiness. God knows how many mistakes I've made over the years! If some of what I have learned can help you experience a more abundant life, though, it would be an honor to share that with you. Remember, what God does for one, He'll do for another; if I've seen God's grace and assistance through His Word, so can you.

I truly believe you have a calling upon your life that is beautiful, powerful, and personal. Each of us do, but we have to fight for it. The enemy wants to convince you to give up because he knows how good your life can be and how much good your life can accomplish.

When you find yourself stumbling or falling, the Bible should be your first recourse. It is objective, unchanging, practical, and powerful. When the temptation to quit comes, you need to fight back. Paul said the Word of God is a sword (Ephesians 6:17), which means it is an effective weapon in times of difficulty. In a letter to Timothy, referring to prophetic words spoken over him, he said "Use those words as weapons in order to fight well" (1 Timothy 1:18 GNT).

God gives us words to fight with, words to rely on, words to overcome. Don't rely just on logic and willpower: find solid truths in the Bible and stand on them. The devil will back down if you persevere, just like he did when Jesus resisted him during the wilderness temptations.

I would not have been able to stand throughout my life without the Bible, and specifically, without the verses below and others God has used to strengthen me in times of need. Each of these truths has meant so much to me. They have kept me in the fight through all the giants of self-doubt, all the fears, all the betrayals, all the disappointments, all the times of lack, all the work. There are so many examples and stories in the Bible of people standing firm in Jesus. Let's look at a few.

CHOOSE TO FOLLOW

These words of Jesus to His disciples have changed my life: "If anyone would come after me, let him deny himself and take up his cross and follow me" (Matthew 16:24). He was referring to people who wanted to be His followers, or disciples. The statement applies to us today. We've got to make a decision. Are we going to be disciples or not? Are we going to be followers?

I had to make a decision years ago that I was going to be a disciple. I wasn't just playing around, and I wasn't just in it to see what I could get out of it—I was going to follow Jesus. I was committed. I decided I wasn't going to treat Jesus like He's the spare tire in my car. You never look at your spare until you get a flat. You don't think about it or care about it. Then when you're stuck on the side of the road, you pull out the spare tire as your last resort. Jesus isn't the spare tire of my car. He's the driver.

Jesus said, "come after me." That means we go where He is. He leads, and we follow. It seems self-evident, but it's so easy to get that backward in life.

Then He said, "deny himself." The word *deny* means to *disown or renounce yourself and submit all your works, all your interests, and all your enjoyments to Him*. That's quite a decision to make.

The next part is what really grabbed me, though. What does "Take up his cross" mean? Before I studied this passage in detail, I had heard the religious teaching that your cross was basically something God gives you that you have to put up with. So, God makes you sick, or He gives you a lousy spouse, or He has your dog run over. Somehow that is "your cross to bear." That doesn't make sense on any level. God's not like that, first of all; and second, Jesus already bore the cross for us. We can't add to His work by carrying more pain. What we do is simply identify ourselves or unite ourselves with Him. We accept

His work, and we align our lives with Him.

By now you know I have to look up words in the dictionary. One way "take up your cross" could be translated is this: *take a stand.* So Jesus was saying, "If you're going to follow me, you're going to have to take a stand." Here's the Charles Nieman translation: "I'm going to have to dig my heels in. I'm not going to back up or back down. I'm taking a stand. I'm burning the white flag."

STILL STANDING

Another verse that has guided my life also talks about taking a stand. Ephesians 6:13 says, "Therefore take up the whole armor of God, that you may be able to withstand in the evil day, and having done all, to stand firm." I've decided in my life that I'm going to stand for something. I'm not going to wait for someone else to tell me what I stand for. I'm going to decide who I follow, and I'm going to take a stand. I'm going to be counted with Him.

At the end of his life, Joshua told Israel they would have to choose which god they would serve. Then he said, "As for me and my house, we will serve the Lord" (Joshua 24:15). He was taking a stand, and he told Israel they needed to take a stand as well.

One of the first things you have to do is decide to take a stand for what you believe. "I'm a Christian, and I'm not apologizing for it. This is who I am, this is what I believe in, and this is how I'm going to live. This is what we're going to stand for in this house and in this family. This is the kind of marriage we strive for, and these are the things we teach our children. This is the way we're going to live. This is the way we're going to approach life. This is what we're going to do with our money. This is what we're going to do with our priorities. I'm taking a stand!"

This was hard for me, because up until the moment I decided to take a stand for Jesus, I hadn't taken a stand on very many things. I was swayed by a lot of opinions. As a kid, because we moved so much, I always had to fit into friend groups that were already established. A lot of kids had known each other since kindergarten, but I would only be there for a few weeks or months—then the assignment for my dad would end, and we would be transferred somewhere else. As a result, I found myself wanting to be included and wanting to be liked. The easiest thing to do was to wait around and see which way the common opinion was flowing, and say, "I agree with that," even if I didn't.

This carried on past my childhood years into adulthood. Then I came headlong into this relationship with Jesus, and it was like He looked at me in love and said, "I'm telling you straight up, if you're going to follow me, you're going to have to take a stand. There's going to be lot of pressure on you to quit, to compromise, to cave in, to not live right, to live right on Sunday morning and not live right on Sunday night. You must take a stand."

Sometimes in my life when I've wanted to wave the white flag, I've remembered this verse and said to myself and my circumstances, "I'm taking a stand. I'm here and I'm not moving. My flag is not white. His banner over me is love. I'm standing firm."

BUY THE PEARL

Here's another Bible passage that absolutely rocked my world when I read it. These two verses have brought me to an incredible determination in my life. Jesus said, "Again, the kingdom of heaven is like a merchant in search of fine pearls, who, on finding one pearl of great value, went and sold all that he had and bought it" (Matthew 13:45-46).

When I read that passage years ago, it resonated with me, and I couldn't shake it. I remember thinking about it for days. I would go to bed at night thinking about it, and I would wake up in the morning thinking about it. I remember wondering, "Do I feel that way about my relationship with Him and my walk with Him? Is Jesus my pearl of great price? Or am I still looking? Do I still think there are other pearls out there, or is He my pearl of great price? Am I willing to stop searching right here?"

This is powerful because pressure comes to leave Jesus, to leave His church, to leave the Word and to go to something else that Satan is telling you is better. It's the classic trick he pulled with Adam and Eve in the garden. Remember, God had placed them in the Garden of Eden, literally defined as "the garden of pleasure," and He told them they could eat everything but the fruit of one tree (Genesis 2:15-17). And they ate that fruit (Genesis 3:6). They had not decided that they had found the pearl of great price in God, so they went looking somewhere they shouldn't have.

I have decided that I have found my pearl of great price. When temptation comes to me, I can say, "No, thank you. I've found my pearl of great price."

"What about this?"

"Nope. I have found my pearl of great price."

"What about that?"

"No, no. I have found my pearl of great price."

"Yeah, but these people think this."

"I don't care what they think. I have found my pearl of great price."

"You are too narrow-minded. You are too constricted. You are missing out."

"Whatever. I have found my pearl of great price, and I'm not leaving it. I'm not searching for something else."

I think all of us, to some degree, are on a search. We are looking for what is truly valuable, truly important, truly worth giving our lives for. When you find your pearl of great price, don't leave it for anything.

NOWHERE ELSE TO GO

Let's look at John 6:66-69. I saw these verses years ago and they stuck with me. Jesus was at an interesting point in His life. He had gained a lot of popularity really quickly, probably because everyone wanted to follow someone who could multiply food and feed thousands. But then He started teaching about what it really meant to follow Him, and that was hard for some people to hear.

Verse 66 says, "After this many of his disciples turned back and no longer walked with him." I've often wondered what those people thought later. They had the opportunity to walk with Jesus, and for some reason they went back. I wonder what they went back to that was better than what they were experiencing with Jesus. Obviously, they had not decided to take a stand. They did not think

He was the pearl of great price.

Verse 67 says, "So Jesus said to the twelve, 'Do you want to go away as well?'" It was a real question. I'm sure the disciples had noticed all the people leaving. They were surely doing some soul-searching themselves. Some of those who were leaving probably tried to talk the disciples out of staying, "This guy's a little weird, Peter. Maybe you should go back to fishing." But the next verse records their reply, and I love it. "Simon Peter answered him, 'Lord, to whom shall we go? You have the words of eternal life'" (John 6:68). It's the same for us. Where else can we go? Once we've known the love and life found in Jesus, nothing else is attractive. Yes, the road ahead seems difficult at times; and yes, there are pressures and problems along the way. But what other option do we have? Jesus has the words of eternal life. Why would we ever turn back to things that are temporary and unfulfilling?

I'VE TASTED THE WATER

John 4 is one of the great chapters of the Bible, in my opinion. In this chapter we see Jesus at a well, talking with a Samaritan woman. He asked her for water, and that started a fascinating conversation.

At one point, Jesus said to the woman, "If you knew the gift of God, and who it is that is saying to you, 'Give me a drink,' you would have asked him, and he would have given you living water" (verse 10). A few verses later, He says, "Whoever drinks of the water that I will give him will never be thirsty again. The water that I will give him will become in him a spring of water welling up to eternal life" (verse 14).

Jesus was talking about Himself. Water symbolizes life. He was telling the woman that once she knew who He was and believed in Him, she would never thirst again, because she would find true, abundant, eternal life in Him.

I don't know how to say it other than this: I've tasted the living water, and I'm not interested in drinking another water. I've tasted and seen that the Lord is good, as the psalmist said (see Psalm 34:8). I've tasted the water of peace, the water of forgiveness, the water of unconditional love. The other waters that are flowing in the earth do not intrigue me. I'm not going to leave living water and go drink some other water.

We have to determine in our hearts that He gives us living water. Just like the parable of the pearl of great price we looked at earlier, we need to realize the value of what we have in front of us. Don't trade living, eternal water for anything this world offers. Don't trade the invaluable for the valueless.

TOUGHEN UP

I already mentioned that I regularly tell myself, "Toughen up, buttercup!" There is a passage in the Bible that says basically the same thing, only it sounds a bit more . . . biblical:

> Be sober-minded; be watchful. Your adversary the devil prowls around like a roaring lion, seeking someone to devour. Resist him, firm in your faith, knowing

> that the same kinds of suffering are being experienced by your brotherhood throughout the world. (1 Peter 5:8-9)

At times in my life when the self-doubts, the betrayals, or some other thing would start to get to me, God would remind me of this verse. I often tell myself, "Grow up, Charles. Things like this happen to everybody. You're not the only Christian in the world who's being persecuted. You're not the only one dealing with things that aren't working out right. You're not the only one who has been disappointed or hurt. It happens to everybody. Quit feeling sorry for yourself. Take your thumb out of your mouth, stand up, and get out of your corner."

That's the conversation I've had to have with myself more than a few times. I don't talk to other people that directly, but I have a pretty good relationship with myself. I know how to motivate me.

This passage reminds me that I'm not the only one facing tests, trials, and tribulations. That's important because the devil tries to tell me, "Nobody has it as bad as you. You poor thing. You are such a sweet pastor. You're just trying to help people. This isn't right. It's not fair. Why don't you go home tonight and get drunk. You'll feel better." Not interested in that. Been there, done that, and got calluses on my knees from puking into the toilet. It doesn't get you anywhere. It just makes your life worse. We have to make the decision to stand firm and not give in to falling, not even when we have a hard day.

LABORERS TOGETHER

Here's another verse that lives in my mind: 1 Corinthians 3:9, "For we are laborers together with God" (KJV). We are all co-laborers, and we work with and for God. If I quit, what am I going to tell the boss, God? What am I going to tell my co-workers, other believers?

I can imagine Jesus showing up at the construction site tomorrow, and I'm not there. "Where's Charles? He was laboring together with me."

To me, one of life's greatest privileges is that we work together with Him. What would I say? "Jesus, it just got so hard."

And He'd show me His hands and His side. "It got hard, Charles?"

Don't get me wrong: Jesus doesn't look down on our suffering. The opposite is true: He understands our suffering, because He's been there. He made it through, and He tells us we can, too.

When I think about all God has done for me, and when I think about the incredible privilege it is to work together to build His kingdom and serve people, I always get my courage back. I get my grit back.

BE A BUILDER

1 Corinthians 3:10 changed my life as well: "According to the grace of God given to me, like a skilled master builder I laid a foundation." In Matthew 16:18, Jesus said, "I will build my church." The Lord is a builder. And I'm predestined, and you are predestined, to be conformed to His

image (Romans 8:29), which makes us builders, too.

I made up my mind years ago that I was going to be a builder, and I remind myself of this just about every day. I tell myself regularly, usually in the morning, "I'm a builder. I'm not a destroyer. I'm not a critic. I'm not here to hurt people. I'm here to build people. I'm not here to make fun of people or beat people up. I'm here to encourage. I'm here to lift people up. I'm going to build up my wife. I'm going to build up my children. I'm going to build my up my grandkids. I'm going to build my friends. I'm going to build the church. I'm a builder."

I think that was one of the greatest decisions I've ever made in my life. When I wake up in the morning, I make a choice. "I'm a builder. I may not have control over a lot of things going on in my life, but I can determine that I'm going to build something worthwhile. I'm going to build up people around me today."

I tell this to our staff all the time. In fact, backstage in our auditorium, there are some big doors that separate the stage from the back hallway. I wrote on the doors with chalk, "We are building something here."

To wave the white flag means you don't want to build anymore. Life is too hard. It's not worth it. I know that feeling, and what gets me up a lot of times is the fact I've decided to be a builder.

What empowers us to be builders? God has a hope and a future for me, and He has one for you. The devil wants us to quit on God's hope and future and go back. He wants us to turn in our resignation. But what we are building is far more eternal than the temporary pressures and pains we face.

How do you know if you're quitting rather than building? What does it look like to wave the white flag as a builder (if you'll excuse the mixed metaphor)? First, you are in danger of waving the white flag when you *settle for managing*. It might not feel like full-on surrender, but it amounts to the same thing eventually. When you become a manager, you are not building anymore. You're just taking care of something, hoping to maintain it, but you're not building it. If that's you, I can hear the flag flapping over your head. You know you are managing when your thinking gets smaller. You are managing when you are okay with okay.

Second, you are in danger of waving the white flag when you start *making excuses* about why you can't build. Do you know what excuses are? Excuses are the flavored syrup the devil gives you so you can swallow quitting. It's like the stuff they put in the medicine at the pharmacy so your kids will drink it. Excuses are the syrup the devil gives you so quitting doesn't taste so bad going down.

Third, you're in danger of waving the white flag when you start *blaming other people*. I've discovered in my life that you've got to own what you do. Yes, people, institutions, governments, and even churches make mistakes. But we're still builders. We can still do our thing.

There's always somebody to blame. At some point, you just have to own your life. You have to say, "It doesn't matter what they think. What matters is what I think. It doesn't matter what they did. What matters is how I respond to what they did. It doesn't matter what they tried to do to me. What matters is what I'm going to do with God right here, right now. I'm going to go build something to the glory of God."

Those are a handful of the Bible passages that have kept me fighting, conquering, and standing strong in the Lord for most of my life. How about you? What are your fighting words? What Bible verses has God used to build strength and courage into your soul? Guard those words, meditate on them, and live them. They will be there when you need them the most.

Are there areas where you are struggling and need a word from God? I would encourage you to read the Bible and make it personal. Study Proverbs if you need wisdom. Study Psalms if you need healing in your soul. Study the gospels if you want to know Jesus better. Study the epistles of the New Testament if you want to learn about Christian living. Study the historical books of the Old Testament if you want to learn from the lives of the faith heroes of old.

God is faithful, and if we seek Him, He will give us the weapons we need to withstand the enemy and stand strong to the end.

ELEVEN

RESTORATION

GOD'S PROMISES AND ABUNDANT LIFE

So far, we've looked at the ways we need to fight in order to run this race, our Christian walk, with faith and endurance. It is important for us to take an active role in our faith, but the Christian walk is not just about fighting. As you walk with God, He will restore you. As you fight, He will restore you.

Earlier, I talked about the difficult season our church went through many years ago. We faced false accusations, financial difficulty, and lack of growth, and I really had to struggle against discouragement. That period lasted for *years*. It wasn't just a hard day, month, or year. It was a hard season, one that I wondered if I'd ever get through. At the time, it felt like we were losing everything, like there was no hope for the future.

That feeling of loss is a very real part of the human experience. Maybe it's happened to you. Things were going well, the future was exciting—and then the bottom seemed to fall out of your dreams. How do we deal with loss? How do we keep from waving the white flag when we are grieving something important to us?

There is a passage in the book of Joel, one of the prophetic books in the Old Testament, that has helped me tremendously in times of loss. This little book, written hundreds of years before Jesus was born, has some of the greatest prophecies in the Bible about Jesus and the church. Peter quoted from one of them in the book of Acts, right after the Holy Spirit came upon the disciples and other believers, to explain to the Jews why all the disciples were suddenly full of the Holy Spirit. The original prophesy in Joel 2 has a lot to do with loss, devastation, and sorrow, but mostly it has to do with *restoration*. It is a promise we can hold on to when we find ourselves facing difficult times. Joel 2:23 says:

> Be glad, O children of Zion, and rejoice in the Lord your God, for he has given the early rain for your vindication; he has poured down for you abundant rain, the early and the latter rain, as before.

Zion in Old Testament prophecy often refers to the people of God. The church, the fellowship of believers worldwide, is God's people under the New Covenant established by Jesus. That's why Peter could quote this prophecy in relationship to the new work God was doing among the believers. Hebrews 12:22 talks about this when it says, "You have come to Mount Zion and to the city of the living God."

Before Jesus, Israel was the people of God; but in

Jesus, that identity and citizenship were extended to believers everywhere. Jesus became the head of the church, and when we believe in Him, we become part of God's people and therefore heirs of those promises, as well. Peter called us "a chosen people, a royal priesthood, a holy nation, God's special possession" (1 Peter 2:9 NIV). Paul declared that we are "fellow heirs, members of the same body, and partakers of the promise in Christ Jesus through the gospel" (Ephesians 3:6).

Many of the things God promised Israel as a nation were fulfilled in their history, and I believe many will still be fulfilled. But the promises go beyond a political nation. As the church, God's promises will be fulfilled in us, as well. He is committed to His people, to all who are called by His name, and we can rest on the promises of His Word.

In Joel's prophecy, he told us to be glad and rejoice because God was going to give us rain. In the Bible, *rain* is often used figuratively to represent *blessings and times of joy*. I believe God wants us to have this mindset and level of faith even when we are going through tough times: He is going to give us blessing and joy.

The prophesy continues. "The threshing floors shall be full of grain; the vats shall overflow with wine and oil" (Joel 2:24). In that agricultural society, this was a declaration of provision and prosperity. God was saying, "I'm going to fill your bank account. I'm going to bring in clients. I'm going to bless your business ventures."

It's the next two verses that really speak to me, though. Here is what they say:

> I will restore to you the years that the swarming locust has eaten, the hopper, the destroyer, and the cutter, my great army, which I sent among you. You shall eat in plenty and be satisfied, and praise the name of the LORD your God, who has dealt wondrously with you. And my people shall never again be put to shame. (verses 25-26)

You have to study this a little to understand what it means, because it's poetic prophecy. These images and terms would have meant something specific to the original hearers. When I first read it, I thought, *Swarming locusts, hopping locusts, destroying locusts, cutting locusts? I'm not a farmer. What does that mean? What does that have to do with me?* But I knew God wanted me to understand something here, so I kept praying about it and studying it.

It was that first phrase that stood out to me the most. "I will restore to you." God is a personal God, and He is a restoring God. In times of loss and lack, God wants us to remember that He has promised restoration. We don't give in to discouragement because we know the future is better than the present.

You might have areas in your life that are like locked rooms in a house. They are rooms that are locked emotionally because there's too much hurt in there, too much loss in there. I'm not asking you to open those doors right now, but I do want you to entertain the possibility that God could restore what's in those rooms.

In the Old Testament, the word *locust* can refer to

a literal locust or it can represent *a season of devastation.* In this passage, although the term referred to an actual locust plague that the land had recently suffered, it also had a wider meaning. It was talking about God's plan to restore the devastation His people had suffered on many levels. Locusts represent many of the things we've talked about in this book: apathy, weariness, temptations, discouragement, deception, distractions, and opposition.

One thing I've discovered about locusts is that they can appear suddenly and disappear just as suddenly. You may have experienced this. You wake up one morning, and you are as happy as you can be; but by the time you get back to your house at night, you wish that day had never happened. Your life can go from great to horrible very quickly. Whatever caused the devastation moves on, but the damage is still there. You survey your life and wonder if you can ever find happiness and wholeness again. If you've felt that, this verse is for you. This promise is for you. God will restore the years the devastation took and the locusts have eaten.

Next, the prophet Joel jumped into an entomology lesson: "the swarming locust . . . the hopper, the destroyer, and the cutter" (Joel 2:25). This was the part that confused me the most, so I studied the meaning of these words. I discovered that the terms *hopper* and *destroyer* refer to growth periods of the locust. The hopper is the stage of the locust when it's not winged yet. It just creeps and hops along the ground. The destroyer is the next stage of locust development. This locust would wreak havoc everywhere it went, devouring everything in its path.

I realized God was saying that no matter where you

are in your loss, He will restore. Maybe you are at the beginning of the devastation, or midway through the devastation, or trying to recover from the devastation. God says, "It doesn't matter where you may be in loss or devastation or hurt. It doesn't matter if it's already occurred or it's only just beginning. Believe for restoration, beginning right now. Don't wait until the locust reaches full stage. Whether it's in the crawling stage or the destroying stage, believe for restoration to begin in your life."

The last kind of locust was the cutter. This wasn't the kind of locust that destroyed everything—it just *affected* everything. You might have a cutting locust at work in your life. You might convince yourself to live with it because it's not eating everything up. It's not destroying your business; it's just hindering your business. It's not destroying your marriage; it's just affecting your marriage. It's not destroying your relationships; it's just limiting your relationships. It's gnawing at your life. But God said, "I'm even going to restore what that cutting locust has destroyed."

I think God spoke about the cutting locust in there to tell us something. We have things in our lives that we think aren't that big of a deal. We might even say, "I don't want to bother God about it." But our prayers never bother God. Our Heavenly Father is not like a human being—up one day and down the next. When we bring something to Him, He wants to hear from us. He wants us to come boldly to the throne of grace (see Hebrews 4:16). He wants us to ask Him to bring restoration to our lives. You are not bothering God. Don't wait for the situation to get bigger. Why not deal with it now? Why not ask God to bring restoration?

God mentioned an army in Joel 2:25, an army that comes against you to bring devastation. That word *army* means *those who are strong for war*. You may have encountered these kinds of people in your day-to-day life. They want to fight, and they will pick a fight. They are strong for war. They use numbers, they use money, they use threats, and they use intimidation to try to bring devastation. But God says, "I will restore even what that army—those people strong for war who came and waged war on you—took away from you. Only believe in me."

God wasn't done yet. He continued, "You shall eat in plenty and be satisfied, and praise the name of the Lord your God, who has dealt wondrously with you. And my people shall never again be put to shame" (verse 26). That phrase *eat in plenty* means, *You will lay claim to the space you once had*. That's the first thing you have to do. The locust may have come and eaten a part of your life, but you're going to take that back. And it's going to be better than it was when it was taken from you. When you hear things like this, doubt might begin creeping up against you. It might start screaming in your head, *How is God going to do this for me?* I'll tell you what I do. I tell my doubt to shut up. I quit worrying about it. I do the believing, and I let God take care of the how. You have to let God be God. I don't know how He's going to do it for you, but can you believe He's capable? Can you believe He wants to?

God said, "you shall be *satisfied*." This is such a fantastic word. It means *you will be filled*. It means *you will have too much*. There's one story in the New Testament where Peter, after fishing all night without catching anything, obeyed Jesus' command to try fishing once more—and he caught so many fish he couldn't take them all into the boat. That's your God. He wants to give you more than enough, but you might have to try one more time. He wants to give you an abundant life.

That word *satisfied* also means *you will enjoy His presence*. Maybe you're saying, "Charles, I have a locked room. I don't even want to go in there. I don't even know if I can. It hurts too badly, and there's too much pain there. I lost too much." Remember, you're not alone. God is right there with you. You're in His presence. Let His love, His light, and His comfort bring restoration.

Verse 26 says that you will "praise the name of the LORD your God, who has dealt wondrously with you." God is telling you to shift your focus from the locust to the Lord. Stop focusing on the devastation and loss, and instead focus on the source of healing and hope. It's so easy to keep your attention fixed on what the enemy has stolen from you, but that doesn't help you at all. God already has a plan in motion to restore and redeem; just keep your eyes on Him.

That word *wondrously* means *extraordinary*. "He has done something extraordinary with you." Restoration is extraordinary! It makes you and those around you take notice. Loss is all too frequent in life, but restoration is a miracle. It is public proof that God is with you and for you.

Finally, God says that you "shall never again be put to shame" (verse 26). The word *ashamed* means you will never *be disgraced or found guilty*. And the word *never* means neither *looking forward or looking backward*. God is saying, "Because I restore you, you won't be disgraced or found guilty looking forward or looking backward."

Most of us are hoping we won't do anything in the future that brings us shame or guilt, but there are things in our past that already do. When God restores us, though, our past is no longer a source of shame, and our future is no longer a source of fear. We are not afraid of future failures or disgraced by past failures, because our lives are restored and hidden in Him.

Believe your past is restored, and believe your future is secure in God. No more regret. No more fear. Burn the white flag of surrendering to the guilt and shame of your past, and burn the white flag of surrendering to the locusts standing in the way of God's promise. You are too important, too valuable, and too loved by God to give up. Stay in the fight! You'll be so glad you did.

NOTE TO THE READER

In order to fight the good fight with endurance and faith, you will need grit, perspective, courage, confidence, joy, vision, growth, truth, and the resolve to stand firm. It might sound like a lot, but God gives you everything you need, and He is with you through it all.

I believe with all my heart God has called you. He has given you the gifts, grace, resources, and opportunities you need to succeed and to live the abundant life. If you will choose to burn the white flag and work toward these things, nothing can stop you. It will be hard, but it will be worth it.

God's Word is your weapon to fight. Become a person of the Word. It doesn't take a theology degree to understand the Bible. It just takes a humble and diligent heart. You'll never exhaust the Scriptures. They are always fresh and always alive. You'll meet Jesus on the pages of the Bible, and you'll find courage to carry on.

Prayer is another key to your success. My wife and I fell in love talking on the phone. She lived eight thousand miles away while we were getting to know each other, and we would often spend two hours a day on the phone. Communication was the foundation of our relationship. In the same way, prayer builds your relationship with God. Just as David strengthened himself in the Lord, so you can find strength in your walk with Him.

Finally, the church is a community of believers, of people just like you and me, who will help you through the tough times. No church is perfect, no leader is perfect, and no Christian is perfect. That is precisely why we need each other. The Bible encourages us to not forsake meeting together (Hebrews 10:25). Jesus told us that where two or three meet together, He is there with them (Matthew 18:20). If you are not connected to a strong local church, I would encourage you to find one. And don't just attend on Sundays. Meet people. Make friends. Become a builder. It will change your life, and it will sustain you if you ever feel too weak to carry on alone.

I hope the stories and principles I've shared in this book have strengthened and encouraged you. Now it's up to you! God is calling you to run the race, fight the fight, and stand firm to the end. No one else can do it *for* you, but God will do it *with* you, every step of the way. Burn the white flag!

ENDNOTES

WORD DEFINITIONS

English word definitions are paraphrased by the author based on the Random House Dictionary. Random House Webster's Unabridged Dictionary. 2001. New York: Random House Reference.

All of the New Testament Greek definitions throughout the book are paraphrased by the author from The Complete Word Study Dictionary: New Testament Zodhiates, Spiros. The Complete Word Study Dictionary: New Testament. Chattanooga, TN: AMG Publishers, 1994.

All of the Old Testament Hebrew definitions throughout the book are paraphrased by the author from The Complete Word Study Dictionary, Old Testament Baker, Warren, and Eugene E. Carpenter. The Complete Word Study Dictionary: Old Testament. Chattanooga, TN: AMG Publishers, 2003.

WORKS CITED

1. "Dr. Whitney Smith." The Flag Research Center. June 27, 2017. Accessed May 28, 2019. https://flagresearchcenter.org/about-the-center/dr-whitney-smith/.

2. Koerner, Brendan, and Brendan Koerner. "Why Do Surrendering Soldiers Wave White Flags?" Slate Magazine. March 21, 2003. Accessed May 28, 2019. https://slate.com/news-and-politics/2003/03/why-do-surrendering-soldiers-wave-white-flags.html.

3. "Dogged." Dictionary.com. Accessed May 28, 2019. https://www.dictionary.com/browse/dogged.

4. Jocko Willink and Leif Babin. *Extreme Ownership: How U.S. Navy SEALs Lead and Win*. St. Martin's Press 2013.

5. William Sanday, Arthur C. Headlam. *A Critical and Exegetical Commentary on the Epistle to the Romans*; T&T Clark, 1901.

6. "Fatigue Makes Cowards of Us All: Why Your Ligaments Should Be Scared." Sparta Science. Accessed May 28, 2019. https://www.spartascience.com/resources/fatigue-makes-cowards-of-us-all-why-your-ligaments-should-be-scared.

7. Brené Brown. *Rising Strong: How the Ability to Reset Transforms the Way We Live, Love, Parent, and Lead*. Random House 2017. Quote edited for context.